An Apprenticeship to Life

An Apprenticeship to Life © Copyright 2004 by Harry J. Bannister

All rights reserved. No part of this work may be reproduced or stored in an information retrieval system (other than for purposes of review) without prior written permission by the copyright holder.

A catalogue record of this book is available from the British Library

First Edition: March 2004

ISBN: 1-84375-092-9

To order additional copies of this book please visit:
http://www.upso.co.uk/harrybannister

Published by: UPSO Ltd
5 Stirling Road, Castleham Business Park,
St Leonards-on-Sea, East Sussex TN38 9NW United Kingdom
Tel: 01424 853349   Fax: 01424 854084
Email: info@upso.co.uk   Web: http://www.upso.co.uk

An Apprenticeship to Life

by

Harry J. Bannister

UPSO

ACKNOWLEDGMENTS

I am grateful to Albert Price for the illustrations in his two editions of 'Blitz on Britain 1939-45'. These enabled me to confirm my memories of my escapade on the weekend of the 15th to the 18th of August 1940. At Cuckmere Haven it is easy to imagine the German bombers flying at zero height on their way to Kenley Airfield, stirring indeed.

I am grateful to my wife Nora for relating her memories of the Blitz during the days of her youth.

I am also grateful to my daughter Linda, for without her delving into the past I would not have known where my ancestors lived. Since at least 1765 they have all been Londoners, some of them Cockneys.

Although I wrote the initial document in 1975 it is now published after the 3rd re-write.

This small volume will, I hope, rekindle memories of those of my generation and will enable the prime evidence written within to give some glimpse to my grandchildren and others of what grandad did in the mid-war years and during the years of the second world war.

A special credit goes to my uncle, James Robert Rogers whose inspiration during my childhood and his great interest in my well being, made it possible for me to grow up in his footsteps. I like to think that I have been his clone, but alas that has proved to have been too large a task.

FOREWORD

AN APPRENTICESHIP TO LIFE

This is the story of a London boy's life, from 1928 when he was three years old until he was called up for war service in November 1943. It is the story of an ordinary lad with all the heartbreaks and humour, that life in a large city brings.

It has tales of his family, his friends, his good parts and his bad parts, and above all the companionship that is peculiar to South Londoners, especially in Lambeth. It tells of the brand of humour that costs nothing and was simple, without harm, and was so different to that of post war London. There were no television broadcasts, and few cars, yet life was full with little time for boredom, and under our very noses history was being made and remembered.

Perhaps the judge of a good life is the amount that can be remembered of ones youth; can much be remembered of life in post war years? History is about people, history is people, stories of recent historical life are scarce, and it is hoped that this book will help to fill this gap.

The author relates his part played during the bombing of London in 1940 and 1941, it includes fire watching duties and service in the Home Guard. Basically it is the story of life in South London of one of it's population, who was then, not highly educated, one of the rough and readies in his young days, but never a hoodlum, perhaps just a scallywag at heart.

An ever muttering prisoned storm,
The heart of London beating warm.
John Davidson.

Woodchurch, Kent
1975, re-written 2003

CHAPTER 1

EARLY MEMORIES

What is the definition of apprenticeship? Dictionaries state that it is one who is learning a craft, and is bound by agreement to serve an employer for a specified time in return for instruction.

Taking authors licence it can be imagined that a young London lad was learning a craft, the craft of how to live and survive in a large city. He is bound to his parents for a specified time who return to him instruction based on their experiences of life, even if some of the instructions turned out to be so wrong. Such is life; anything learned the hard way is never forgotten.

One of the best assets to any apprentice is a good memory; my earliest memory is of Cimex Lectulsrius, the common bed bug. It has been recorded that in 1939 there were 4,000,000 people living in London troubled by these insects, in 1928 I was one of the earlier unfortunates. Born in 1925 in Camden Town, a district of St Pancras, I realised at an early age that bugs were a persistent part of a way of life, disappearing by day and emerging at night.

The habitat of the bugs was the broken plaster and multi layers of wall paper, that lined the walls of rooms in the slum houses we lived in, they also lived in the rotting wood of architrave's and skirting boards. It was hazardous to remove the wallpapers, as it was often the only support in holding the plaster to the walls, I remember my father once removing seven layers from a wall.

My father was badly wounded at Ypres in the First World War, in 1928 he still had a weeping wound. He had a quick cure for all bed bugs, along with most Londoners in those days we had a 'gosunder' or chamber pot under the bed, on his return from the local pub, always the worse for drink, he prepared for bed. He always had a call of nature, then with a half filled pot he would wander around the room, and dressed only in his long johns he would deftly flick the insects into the pot. He always chuckled with every 'score'. How did I know this? We all slept in the same room; we only had two, one for sleeping and one for living in. Father used the pot rather than stagger down four flights of stairs, the lavatory was at the end of the back yard, and with 22 people in the house there was always the chance that someone would be in the 'privy'. By the time father had climbed the stairs he would want to use the pot once more. He had a dread of stairs when he was inebriated, no doubt due to the many falls he had in the past, obviously we had the largest pot available. When the pot was full, father emptied it by simply opening the window and pouring it out (we were on the fourth floor) on to the front garden below, such as that was, nothing grew there for obvious reasons.

Occasionally the fumigation officer called, we had to leave our rooms while he debugged them, he usually did the whole house and we were not allowed back for four hours. We usually went to Aunt Mary who lived across the road, taking some of our bugs with us, but then she was as infected as we were. When we went back bugs were found around the walls on the floor, and especially around the beds. It was a losing battle, and there soon returned another generation of the creatures. The houses were demolished about 15 years ago.

Poor Mrs Smith who was a cut above us 'poors' had moved in only a short while before, and she would not allow her daughters to play with us, alas even her precious daughters succumbed to bug bites, much to our delight.

One thing we seemed not to have were fleas; it was said that if bugs were present fleas were not.

At the age of four an ambulance arrived one day to take me to hospital, I had contracted scarlet fever, this illness was common among children, it was as common as diphtheria and was sometimes fatal, it was treated seriously, and was always a hospital admittance, today these illnesses are seldom heard of.

During my stay in hospital I was inundated with toys from aunts and uncles, one such gift was a lovely set of farm animals, I looked forward to the day when I would leave with my new acquisition, alas it was not to be, all items taken into isolation wards had to be left behind for the enjoyment of other children. This was the first disappointment I can remember.

An Apprenticeship to Life

Another early memory is of socks, the front of our house looked out on the rear of the houses opposite, the house directly opposite was occupied by my maternal grandmother, my aunt Mary, her husband Charley, and my cousins Reggie and Florence, she was rather uppity and would on no account be called Flo. Uncle had feet that anyone with a good nose soon discovered, whenever he came home from work he went straight to his bedroom, removed his socks, opened the window and placed the offending socks on the window sill. He then shut the window on to the socks to prevent them from blowing away to the yard below. My mother used to look across the road and say, "Charley is in, his socks are out". Was this a cure for Bromidrosis that was lost to posterity?

Aunt Mary took in washing, and in an outhouse in her back yard she had a stone sink the like of which I have not seen since then. The sink was 6' feet long, and 4' wide with sides of only 9" high, made from one piece of stone. There was also a boiler made from one piece of stone. It was said that the previous occupier was a fishmonger and that he prepared his wares there.

Uncle Charley lit the boiler fire on Monday before he left for work; there was always a great pile of washing to be done. Along one side of the yard there was a long lean-to with many clotheslines hanging up in order to dry the washing in wet weather. Aunt had a strict routine in her work, on Monday ,Tuesday and Wednesday; she would wash, and iron on Thursday and Friday. Saturday was her delivery day when she loaded her cart with the clean washing and delivered it to the market traders and shopkeepers in Queens Crescent only 10 minutes from her yard.

Her cart was constructed from an old perambulator with a large box with a lid fitted; uncle Charley made this. As she delivered she collected dirty aprons and coats ready to be washed the next week. Sunday was her day 'off', and then she did her housework. I cannot remember her having any time to herself, to me she was rather remote and of few words.

Uncle Charley was the opposite, he was a large ponderous man because of his bad feet, and he would talk to anyone, and would pass his opinion on any subject, quite lucidly.

He was a foreman at the Gaslight and Coke Co, when he was about 50 he was stung by a bee, and never really recovered, he took early retirement to play his concertina which he did rather well.

Cousin Reggie was a bully, at least 18" taller than myself and much heavier, he had a habit of twisting my ear whenever we met, one day, small and young as I was, I jumped up and punched him in his left eye, his eye was troubled for a long time afterwards, but he never bothered me again. Father gave me a good hiding for what I did to 'poor' Reggie; there wasn't much justice in my young life.

One person I have dear memories of was my paternal grandmother; she lived across the road with Aunt Mary, and had a room of her own. She was totally blind, I never knew her able to see, she would sit by her kitchen range all day and seemed very happy with her lot in life. Her room was never cold in winter, a really cosy room for an old person, and she was the only grandparent I ever knew.

When I was 6 years old I often went round to the local public house to get grannies beer, as soon as the pub opened I collected her jug, a quart jug, then went to the Jug bar, this was just around the corner. The bar was commonly called 'The Jug', most pubs had one at that time, it was a tiny bar with barely room for two people at the counter and was only for take away drinks. It served two purposes, the first it enabled old folks to purchase their drinks with out the need to push through a crowd of drinkers, some who may be inebriated, and secondly it enabled the more genteel customer not to have the stigma of being seen in a public house. However, I stood outside until someone who knew me came along, I gave them fourpence and the jug, they gave me the jug full of porter as they came out with their wares. On the way back I would scoop the froth from the beer, I had acquired a taste for it, I would then put the froth back on the beer by stirring it with my finger. Grandmother always mulled her beer, and when I gave the jug to her she would place the jug on the hearth and withdraw the poker (which by then was red hot) from the fire, she would then plunge the poker into the jug with a satisfying hiss. It was amazing how she never burnt her hands, and never missed the jug; after all she was blind. My reward for the beer 'Run' was a thick slice of dripping toast, again it was done without burning her hands, dripping toast has never tasted as good as it did in those days.

In 1932 we moved to Brixton, South London, my uncle Jim rented a house in Strathleven Road, N° 1, the first floor flat had become vacant and he offered it to my father who gratefully accepted. It was at last an escape from the slums to a house free from bugs, to a house where for the first time we had electric light and our own toilet; there was a small scullery which doubled as a bathroom. When a bath was needed a large tabletop was removed from over the bath and replaced afterwards to form a working surface. There was a gas cooker in the kitchen, and the kitchen being a large one also served as the living room. The bedroom, which looked on to the road served as the bedroom for all of us, for me as a young lad it, was utopia.

Mother was well known in the Acre Lane area, she had lived there as a young girl, although she was born in North Lambeth at 15 Cornwall Road only just around the corner from Waterloo Bridge, Aunt Win and Uncle Jim lived on the ground floor of N°1. They were both single, Jim was the oldest member of the family, my favourite and my idol.

There had been many quarrels in the family during my parents life in Camden Town, they had moved there after their marriage on the 28th of April 1924 at Lambeth registry Office, mother was 29 and father 31, I was surprised to find from the marriage certificate that grandfather's second name was Moses, Jewish extraction? no, it was a name that had started many years ago, back in the 16th century; the family was always christened, married and buried from Church of England parishes.

Fathers elder brother Francis lived at harrow and was well off, he was high in management at Odhams Press at Watford.

After a visit to Harrow there was a blazing row which ended with us going home suddenly, much to my disgust, as my cousin had a wonderful model railway, with a terminus in his bedroom, and a tunnel thorough the wall leading to a long run around their garden, truly to my eyes sheer delight.

I have never found out what the row was about, and probably I never will after all these years, I believe it was due to my fathers drinking habit, but whatever the cause it will remain a mystery. Because of the row and also the offer from Uncle Jim the decision was taken to move to Brixton.

I was much happier after we moved, all our belongings were fumigated, including our clothes, we then moved into a nice, freshly painted first floor flat as I have described above. At that time the Brixton house was like a palace to me, and best of all we had left the bugs behind for good.

At the time we moved my brother was 2 years old, I was 7, like myself Leslie had been born in the one large room at Camden Town, little did we know that he had only 3 more years to live, I will relate the story later in another chapter. The room at Camden Town had a large bed, a Victorian bed, of the type that had a large cranked winding handle to tension the springs, in that bed was born my father, myself and my brother, when we moved to Brixton we left the bed behind. In the history of my family that bed was a wondrous piece of furniture.

Mother had been suffering from asthma for many years, she thought it was from years of inhaling paper dust when she worked in the cutting and binding rooms at a firm of printers named Kit-Kat. After we moved she was sent to the London Homeopathic Hospital for treatment, this was always on Mondays at 9am, because there was nobody to look after us we always went with mother. We were up early on those days and mother, Leslie and I walked down Acre Lane to Brixton Town Hall and boarded a 33 Tram, this took us to Westminister Bridge via Kennington, Horns pub (now closed), along the Thames embankment, through the Kingsway tunnel to Great Ormond St. Leslie and I waited about 2 hours for mother, with sweets and drinks from the nurses and returned home with a much improved mother.

I liked the weekly trips, it gave me a day away from school and another ride on a Tram, and Trams gave me great delight, and still do especially foreign ones. The subway tunnel had only been reopened a year, it was originally built for single decker trams and was heightened to accommodate double-deckers. The reopening ceremony was done by a white double decker, it's serial number was 1931 and it was opened in 1931. The tunnel was lined with white tiles throughout, and was well lit. There were three stations, Aldwych, Kingsway and Holborn. In order to alight or board the trams, passengers had to use the exit at the driver's end, and this was because the platforms were between the tracks. As the trams approached the city end of the tunnel there was a steep climb to reach roadway level, and although the trams weighed 27 tons the slope was climbed easily, on those days the tram trip was my highlight of the day. The entry from the southern end was directly underneath the Waterloo Bridge approach where it crossed the Embankment.

Saturday was usually a shopping visit to Brixton market, afterwards mother and aunt Win, (who always went shopping with us) went to the 'Black Horse' pub in Brixton High St, and this pub was a wine house. Leslie and I waited outside until closing time at 3pm, it was safe to play

An Apprenticeship to Life

The white tram.

Holborn Station

there as it had an alley at the side and was away from the main road. The alleyway led between high brick walls to the junction of Coldharbour Lane and Brixton Road. At this point Trams changed over from the conduit system to the overhead system of power supply, Leslie and I thought it was wonderful how the Trams would throw out the collection shoe and how the driver would connect the long overhead pole to the wire. Afterwards we always went to the 'Astoria' cinema in Stockwell road as aunt Win's treat, my first recollection of a film there was Eddie Cantor in 'The Kid From Spain' and Gordon Harker in the 'Frog' series.

Occasionally we went to Waterloo station on a Saturday morning to meet father during his morning break, he worked odd hours, his employer's were W.H.Smith & Son Ltd at their printing works in Stamford Street near Waterloo Bridge. This was strangely only just around the corner from where my mother was born, father was the senior warehouseman and went to work on Wednesday mornings and returned at 6 p.m. his hours were the same for Thursdays. But on Friday he left home at 7 a.m. and returned home on Sunday mornings about 11 a.m. this is the reason why we went to see him on Saturdays, mother and father would sit in the Buffet supping their favourite drink

An Apprenticeship to Life

'Guinness'. This allowed me to roam around the concourse and the platforms armed with a penny platform ticket, my brother usually stayed with mother at the table.

With my ticket I would wander up the platforms, especially N° 1, this was said to have been the longest Platform in the world, nearly one mile long. Unbeknown to me at that time, it was from this platform that my paternal grandfather climbed down to his death on the 2nd of September 1904, as he attempted to climb up on to the opposite platform to greet an old friend he did not hear empty carriages approaching, he was hit and died later at his home. He was drunk at the time. It was certainly a long walk for a small lad to reach the engine that had fourteen coaches behind it. I got to know all the names and numbers of the main line Loco's. One day a driver lifted me onto the footplate of N° 851 'Sir Francis Drake', the dream of most boy's come true, I lost count of the number of times I had gazed in awe at the giants of the Southern Railway, an interest that has stayed with me through the years.

Father's job at Smith's was on the production of a pre-war magazine called 'Everybody's Weekly', the magazine was very popular in the pre-war period, I looked forward to the 'hot from the press' copy father brought home with him on Sunday mornings. Alas the publication became a war casualty and did not survive; it failed to relate to the changing styles of 1946 and after.

Again I digress, I was always late getting back to the Buffet, father often came looking for me, I was not hard to find, he simply asked each platform ticket collector if they had seen the boy with the black and green school cap on his head, most of them knew me. Even today I like to think that I know more than most of the London and Southwestern and the Southern Railway.

I confined myself to the first ten platforms, these were the mainline platforms, and the rest up to 24 were for the suburban routes with unglamorous Loco's.

I always wondered where the trains went, the 'Golden Arrow' and others like it, the world away from London seemed so far away. One day I would fulfil my dream of world travel, but that will be another story.

After father returned to work mother would walk us to the New Cut, which was at the end of Cornwall Road, there was a street market there on Saturdays. I always made haste to a certain second-hand book stall which also sold all sorts of American magazines, the ones I looked for were 'Mechanix Illustrated', these were full of ideas and inventions, I hoarded them and perused them time and time again. I am tempted to believe that these magazines and the car articles led me to an interest that gave me a career and a good living in later years.

I learned much from those around me, especially those who were less fortunate than I, at least fathers good wage fed and clothed us well, our standard of living had certainly improved with our move to Brixton, despite half of his wage being spent on alcohol. Leslie and I were vastly different, he had blond hair and blue eyes and I have black hair and dark brown eyes, he liked girlish toys and I liked mechanical things.

From an early age I can remember putting things together from paper and cardboard, and loved to build the construction sheets that were so popular in the pre war era, there were many types of sheets, castles, houses, and other buildings, quite cheap, from sixpence upwards.

CHAPTER 2

THE APPRENTICESHIP BEGINS – OUR MOVE TO BRIXTON

THE PIANO – CRYSTAL PALACE

There was a way of life in South London that was unique in the British Isles, it was a close warm way of life especially in the Borough of Lambeth.

I quickly became engulfed into this way of life as I grew up, most of this life came from friendships fostered in public houses, the public house was either the poor mans institution or the middle class mans club.

The majority of the pub' regulars saw each other every night of the week including Sundays, they knew of the intimacies and secrets of each others lives and families, their children hardly knew each other unless it was from playing with each other outside a pub', where the parents were drinking inside. Paradoxically they rarely visited each other's homes; in fact they saw more of each other every night than they saw of their own families. One could set the clock by the regularity that my parents had when they walked through the Saloon bar door, it was commonplace for even young children to play and wait outside the pub' each night, I certainly did my share of waiting.

Always after closing time there was at least a half hour chat or a sing song, often finishing their drinks outside and leaving their empty glasses on the window sills, I knew one pub' that had a shelf erected just for 'empties' after closing time. If there were a shortage of glasses at home, a glass or two would find it's way into a handbag or pocket, most of the glasses my parents had bore the mark of the Weights and Measures Department.

Often, on a cold winter night I had wanted to go home to thaw out, only to be told "Wait until we come out", I always knew then that I was in for another cold nights wait. The 'Hope and Anchor' pub' in Acre lane, Brixton, had an inner circular draft curtain inside the door of the Saloon bar, this was useful for me to nip inside and warm up without being seen. Unfortunately the Publican, Fred Farmer, would never have underage persons in the bars, he would go to my father and say "Harry, put your boy outside", he would never break the law, and yet a few minutes later he would bring me out a lemonade or a chocolate bar, he was a most kind man, but to break the law, never.

I often heard people going to the bar say " Harry and Ethel keep their boy well clothed", they had to, otherwise I would have frozen to death. It never occurred to them to spend an evening at home around the fire, in the warm, a pub' was their life and they just had to go out, even if it killed them. In later years it did just that to one of them, in fact alcohol eventually killed both of them. I hope to relate these stories in another book.

The only thing that sustained me during those nights was the Lemonade and arrowroot biscuit, that were brought out to me, often by people I never knew.

My parents became engaged in their local pub, celebrated their Golden Wedding in it, and used it for over 60 years, and yet during that time there were only three publicans who ran it, and two of these were father and son.

The pub' population was finely divided among the local pub's, there was no means to travel to and from the pub's unless one walked, in the area where we lived there were eight within a half-mile of each other. People were reluctant to travel outside their local area unless it was to visit relatives or those classified as old friends rather than as pub' acquaintances. Pub' users were in the main, local people only, any strange person entering a bar would cause much suspicion and speculation. Each local person had their own special place in the bar or usual seat that was left empty until the regular arrived, there tended to be more bars than today. There was the Public bar that the lower income people used, the Private bar was used by the more genteel imbiber, and the single middle aged ladies and widows and old couples who wanted a quiet drink. The Saloon bar was occupied by the middle class of the day or those who could not afford more than one drink but considered themselves a cut above the Public bar, and would sit in a corner all night

An Apprenticeship to Life

with the one drink, hoping someone would 'treat' them. There was a small Off Licence bar from where those who liked to drink at home could buy their choice, without having to go into another bar. Sometimes the Off Licence would be called the Jug bar or just the Jug, this came from past times when beer was bought in jugs.

Passing drinks in the pubs was rampant, my parents had a friend who was a bar-maid at their local, she was a huge busted woman who literally rested on the bar counter, I have never seen any one so large since then. When she was alone in the bar my parents seemed to have drunk twice as much for the same cost, virtually every other drink free. This free trade went on with a number of other customers, and lasted a few years until the publican caught her doing something at the till, there was a blazing row, she walked out and was never seen to serve in the area again. She had worked there for over 20 years; most pubs had their circle of fiddlers.

The publican had absolute power over his customers; there was no fear of reprisal against any order. Any person falling out of acceptance to the landlord was barred; the ban lasted until the person had been punished enough. The wonderful communications that existed enabled the person to be able to enter the pub' without any message being sent. The 'grape vine' was very efficient, when the customer once more appeared in the pub he or she was greeted by the publican like a long lost relative, and as though nothing had ever happened.

My father was banned once because of his amorous overtures to women in the bar when he was silly with drink, he was barred and mother was not, she often went in and left him to go to another pub, such was the pull of the local.

The comradeship was very strong, and no one went wanting for help. Any help was usually in the form of cash from collections within the pub, and for those days large sums were raised.

An illustration of the strength friendship was when my mother died, her funeral was routed past the local pub, at the pub the procession halted, and all the customers came out of the pub onto the pavement and lined up. They raised their glasses and bowed their heads, there were more than 40 of them, and then went back inside to drink her health, so to speak, there were few tears, it was a pause in the day and so life went on. Another of the old girls had gone, she was 84.

Life was so philosophical then as indeed it is still among the old folk, alas they lived in a past world, and they realise this and accept it for what it is. For all the protection they receive today with all the medical benefits that are available, and no matter how hard life had treated them, they are always eager to talk of 'The Good Old Days'.

Father's drink was bottled Guinness, little did I know then that I would in later years hold a Senior position in the Guinness brewery at Park Royal.

I calculated once that up to 1979 he had consumed £12,000 worth of Guinness in his lifetime. Mother was a great Port drinker in her younger days, turning to Guinness in her later years; her brand of Port was Dow's. It was remarkable that although neither of them were educated to any standard, they had a talent for discussing the merits of port and Guinness in fact whenever there was doubt on the quality of a glass of the 'Black' brew he would be asked his opinion. He would sip, think, and then pass judgement, he was seldom wrong, he was the locally accepted exponent of the stout. He claimed that up to the day that he died the drink was not as good as it was in his young day, he would not accept that Liffey water was compatible with park Royal water. I did a test on him at one time, I poured out two glasses from unmarked bottles, one from Dublin and one from London, and he tasted both and told me which was which. Was it a guess? I doubt it, with all my experience on the beer tasting panels and with the many experts, I have never known anyone with his perception of drinking matters.

But there, he had made it his life time study.

The local publican was Fred Farmer, he was a large bluff man, very popular and a pillar of strength in the local area, he was always organising pranks and was a great practical joker.

My Uncle Jim acquired a piano, it was a very heavy Pianola, there came the day to move it in, a Carter knocked on the door, said he had a piano outside and who was going to unload it. Father, uncle Jim and the Carter tried to move it, and found it too heavy, fathers brainwave was to go round to the local pub to seek help from Fred Farmer. Fred gathered help from his customers, most of whom were my fathers drinking cronies, about a dozen appeared, some still with a glass of beer in their hands, most of them came round just to see what was going on. Fred looked at the situation, took charge and said, "get that horse out of the shafts, half a dozen of you tip the cart up and the rest of us will slide it down", and so they did. Unfortunately as the piano dropped to the ground so did the cart, with a crash, this frightened the horse which ran across the road complete with it's nosebag, it kicked out and hit an 'X.L.' chewing gum machine, the front fell off and spread packets of the gum over the pavement.

Poor Mrs Sutclift, who owned the machine that was mounted on the wall outside her sweet shop, opened the door to see what the noise was, she being a nervous, seedy, frail person and being confronted by a horse promptly had a funny turn. Mother and next-door neighbour ran over to comfort her, the horse was caught and was tied to the railings, and the piano was installed on the pavement.

Fred wondered if the piano would still play, he said to my father "come on Harry, give us a tune", father could play a good pub sing song style, Fred sent a couple of lads back for some beer and glasses, father sat on one of Tunesi's apple boxes, (Tunesi was the corner greengrocer) and thumped out a few tunes. Fred offered his straw boater to passers by and collected a nice sum of money for his local charity the NSPCC. The gathering, being on the corner of a main road, Acre lane, attracted the attention of the local 'Bobby'; he turned a blind eye to what had turned out to be a good cause held on a Saturday morning. I stood on the ground floor window sill and watched it all unfold

Fred Farmer was an institution in himself, he had been the publican at the 'Hope and Anchor in Acre lane for many years having taken the pub over from his father, he was a good likeness of 'Wakey Wakey' Bill Cotton. He was very well respected and wore a straw boater the whole year round, and always had a white apron tied around his waist. He treated me kindly with the occasional Arrowroot biscuit or a glass of lemonade sent out to me.

One winter day the saloon bar regulars had a lark at Fred's expense, Fred's boater was used for any collection around the bars, collections were common place. Father, in collaboration with the rest of the customers asked for his boater for a collection, Fred readily obliged, father put the boater on a stool below bar height, out of sight. Father picked up a second old boater, winked at his cronies and said " it's about time Fred had a new hat" the barmaid said" I have been telling him that for years", Fred came over to see what was going on just in time to see my father put his fist through the old boater that he had bought in with him, father then threw the hat on the fire that was always blazing on winter days, Fred jumped over the bar and rescued two remnants of his hat, so he thought. He said " I have had that boater since the end of the War (1918)", he almost sat down and cried until he saw Father standing in front of him wearing his boater, Fred saw the funny side of this jape. This was the kind of rapport that existed in the 1930's.

Fred was always the joker, one New Year's eve the tables were turned on him once again. At midnight the revellers formed a line and went dancing down Acre lane, the road was being widened past the shops toward Brixton town hall, at this point Fred was too inebriated to carry on, the dancers placed him in a wheelbarrow that was taken from the road works, and with a red-light hanging from each end of the barrow he slept peacefully. A passing Police patrol found him in the early hours, and took him to Brixton Police Station to sleep it off. Fred was in disgrace with the Magistrates and with the Brewery (Young's). The charge of causing an obstruction was not proven, and he was discharged. Alas Fred has now become part of the local history, and the area is all the poorer for the loss of his humour.

At times when my father had a Saturday free from work, he took us up to the 'West End'. We would leave the route 24 bus at Parliament Square and walk up Whitehall to Trafalgar Square, then round to Suffolk Street; this is a tiny narrow street at the rear of Cockspur Street. At this point I must digress, whenever I was in this area I had a feeling of something strange, a feeling of belonging there, a warm feeling as if I was being welcomed, and now 67 years onwards I have discovered why I had that feeling. This will be explained at the end of this book. To resume, in Suffolk Street there was a small Pub' that my parents liked, and as usual I waited outside, unusual for me I enjoyed waiting outside this particular Pub', the ulterior motive being ships. There was a lot of shipping offices there, and in the windows there were models of the shipping lines ships. I spent many happy hours gazing at these models. Just down the street from the Pub' there was a window with a beautiful model of a ship, mounted in a glass case, it was about 8' long. As I stood looking at it one day, a man who was sitting at a desk beckoned me in; I opened the door and entered. He said that he had often seen me looking in his window at the ship, and was there anything I would like explained? My questions tumbled out, where did the ships go to, what did they carry, who did they belong to, and many more questions were answered. I left his office after he gave me a coloured brochure of the world's largest ship that had not yet been launched, the year was 1935, and it was to be 'The Queen Mary' later that year. The brochure had 50 pages and was the size of a small newspaper, today it is one of my cherished possessions, albeit now rather tatty. I told father where I had been; he walked back with me to the office and spoke to the man who said I was always welcome. Over the next year or two we became firm friends, he always found time for a friendly word. Father smoked cigars at that time, and each time we went there, he gave me one to give to Mr Bibby as we called him, he was named that because it was on a brass plate on the door, it was probably something to do with the 'Bibby' Line which was a prominent shipping line in the 30's. About the end of 1937 I went to see him, I was told that he did not work there anymore. We never found out where he went or what befell him, the memory of that man has remained with me all my life, he was one of life's kindly persons. I often wonder if he had been an ex-captain, he probably had been just an office receptionist or a shipping clerk. I have always been a dreamer, without dreams the world is not yours. I often thought then of Rudyard Kipling's poem 'Big Steamers', with it's first line; 'Oh, where are you going to, all you Big Steamers'.

I sometimes wandered around Trafalgar Square to gaze at Landseer's lions and to look at Nelson, Hmm, how did they get him up there? Then across the other side of the Square to 'Africa House', why did South Africa want such a big house to itself? If only grown up's had realised that a young boy needed answers to all these questions, but then, as I was always told, " You will have plenty of time to find the answers". Of course the truth was that the grown up's didn't know the answers themselves.

As I look back, I wonder how a young lad of 10/11 years old could wander around London and come to no harm. More so, how could parents have allowed it to happen, it would be unthinkable today, perhaps because it did happen I learned, and knew so much more of life at that age than most youngsters know today. They probably know more about computers and electronic wizardry at ten years old, but is that a good start to learn about life?

Another part of London I wandered around in was the Strand and Fleet Street; my parents used two pubs' in this area, Henekeys and Shorts. Henekeys fronted on to the Strand, almost on the corner of

Wellington Street, the entrance to the bars was up a covered alley which also led to the rear exit from the Lyceum Theatre, I often caught glimpses of the actors when they slipped out for a quick drink during the interval, some of them I remembered from seeing them at the Empress at Brixton.

After being told not to cross the Strand on our visits, I did just that, often, but for one reason only, and that was to see the progress on the new Waterloo Bridge. The temporary bridge had been installed for some time, it was a double girder bridge of a single lane each side, I enjoyed watching the bridge bounce whenever a bus or heavy lorry left the bridge to enter Lancaster Place. The new bridge was finished in 1944, it took over six years to build, the original bridge was built by Rennie and was opened in 1817, but was rather narrow, only 42' 6".

I remember sometimes walking right across Waterloo Bridge just for one purpose, which was to visit two shops. The first was the second shop on the right as one left the bridge at the commencement of Waterloo Road facing south. This shop was a tattooists, gazing through the window I watched people being tattooed, around the shop were beautiful designs and patterns, of course I didn't understand why people were having pictures put on their bodies, no more than I do today I suppose.

The second shop was on the left-hand side, almost opposite the tattooist, this was a gun shop. I once saw a notice on a gun in the window which said 'The hunting gun of Indian Princes', I entered the shop and asked, "What did the Princes hunt?" I was told Tigers and Elephants, the gunsmith gave me a brochure of the gun, and it was a Mannlicher-Schoener. I wondered who would buy the gun and what would they kill, little did I realise then, that in only six years time I would be handling guns equally as powerful as the gun in the window.

After tea on the afternoon of Monday November 30th 1936, our local gang gathered as usual at the corner of Ellerslie Square to decide what to do with the rest of the day. Some of us had heard rumours that there was a big fire at West Norwood, then we heard that the 137 bus was being turned around before it reached Crystal Palace. As the afternoon darkened we could see a red glow in the sky at the end of Kings Avenue toward Streatham. We decided to go and have a look at the fire, we thought the best way to get there would be to skate. We were all proficient skaters and the mile and a half to the end of Kings Avenue would be easy. Unfortunately the fire was not at the end of Kings Avenue, although we were a lot closer to the fire. We asked and were told that it was the Crystal Palace burning. We carried on the remaining two and a half miles, and I was particularly concerned as my Uncle Jim worked at the Palace with John Logie Baird the television pioneer, and made the supports for Baird's apparatus whenever it was required.

When we arrived, the Palace was burning fiercely and well out of control, the parade in front of the Palace was closed, as was the low-level station. Uncle Jim shared a house in Anerley Hill which ran down the south side of the Palace, he stayed there whenever he was working late as he intended to do that evening. I left my friends and skated to the house and was told that he was at the North tower helping to remove some equipment. I went back to try to find him, but police were clearing people from all the roads around the Palace, thousands of people were watching, the crowds were vast, they stood and watched as the enormous building burnt to the ground. As the huge central nave crashed to the ground the noise was heard five miles away. I went back to the house where uncle Jim's friend took me up to the roof to a flat part, and from there we saw the flames gradually die down.

It was Sir Henry Buckland who was the driving force behind the modern Crystal Palace, and it was he who first saw the fire from outside. He had just left his house to cross the road to post a letter when he saw a glow coming from within, he ran inside and found some workmen trying to put out a fire that had started in a small lavatory. It was later thought that a carelessly discarded cigarette had started the fire.

Sir Henry realised that this was more than just a small fire of which there had been many over the years, this one had actually taken hold. He ran to warn some members of an orchestra who were rehearsing at the far end of the building, they ran for their lives, and so quickly did the fire spread that they could not even save their cars. There was a strong wind blowing from the Northwest, and when the flames burst through the transept it became a gigantic funnel.

The alarm had spread to many outside fire brigades, eventually there were 89 appliances attending the site, because of the height of Sydenham Hill water pressure was low, the only parts it was thought could be saved were the two towers and the low level station. Just after 8 o/clock the transept was burning to its full height, wherever the glass melted flames shot through like great columns of fire. At twenty-five

Harry J. Bannister

Souvenir of the Crystal Palace, destroyed by fire, Nov. 30th 1936.

minutes to nine the transept crashed to the ground, flames roared 300 feet into the night sky and then roared into the South nave. The glow was seen over the whole of London, and people as far away as Hampstead watched it burn, an Air-liner pilot said as he was flying over the Channel it appeared that the whole of London was burning. At Brighton people went to Devil's Dyke to see the skyline aglow, they just stood and wondered.

There was a great drifting in of people from all of South London. Every side street that had even just a small glimpse of the fire was packed with people, standing in awe. People were thronging down Anerley Hill, they had smarting eyes and were coughing with smoke in their lungs, and the south tower above them was burning like a torch even though it had a tank at the top containing 1,000 Tons (224,000 gallons) of water. Later Anerley Hill was cleared of people and traffic in case the Tower fell.

All this I watched, as our Palace burnt itself into history, little did we know that in four years time we in London would be dealing with fires that would make this one seem like a garden bonfire.

About 11o/clock Uncle Jim came down Anerley Hill, we were all so very relieved to see him, but he was safe, his face was black, his coat was torn, and he was more dragging than carrying a very large canvas bag. Inside the bag was a flag, the Union Jack that had flown from the pole at the top of the north tower, it was a very large flag, and how he carried it we never knew. He had this flag for many years afterwards, I know not of its whereabouts now, it would have been of great historical value.

An Apprenticeship to Life

Every side street that had even a small glimpse of the fire was packed with people standing in awe.

Uncle Jim telephoned the 'Hope and Anchor' to let my parents know I was safe, yes at half past eleven they were still in the pub', it was halfpast one when we came down from the roof. I slept at Anerley Hill that night, the next morning Uncle Jim and I went round to the Palace. All that was left standing were the two Towers and part of the north nave. The rest of the building had fallen into the basement and was still burning; most of the debris was cordoned off, as it was too hot to walk upon. There was a mountain of iron and twisted girders, great pieces of black glass everywhere. Even the goldfish in the ponds had turned black, but were otherwise unharmed. The crystal fountain had remained intact amidst all this desolation.

Uncle Jim took me home on the 137 bus later in the day, I went back to school the next day with a sick note, which was some what true as I was sick with the thought that the Palace was gone forever. The south tower was demolished a few days later, Uncle Jim took me to see it felled, one loud bang and it was felled very neatly away from Anerley Hill.

The north tower lasted a few months before it too was demolished. So, the glass Palace that had stood on Sydenham Hill since 1854 was no more. No more would I go to the fireworks displays, the dog shows, the music concerts, the circus and the other exhibitions that were held from time to time.

There was a large void left when the Palace had gone, it had been a symbol for the people of London that was never to be replaced, it had become a place for a good day out for the family. The site became a controversy for many years, eventually and ironically the BBC erected an aerial six hundred feet high there. A fitting memorial to John Logie Baird, he would have been delighted to have seen television so advanced, although the system used was not his, I am proud that uncle Jim helped him in his work.

John Logie Baird died in 1946, although the BBC adopted his system in 1929, they abandoned it in 1936. He continued until he died with his experiments in screen projection and stereoscopic colour effects.

It seems a quirk of fate that when the world abandoned his system in 1936, the place where he had pioneered TV so well was burned to the ground in the same year. Today the grounds have regained some of their former popularity.

CHAPTER 3

THE FAMILY – THE POSHER SIDE – THE POORER SIDE

THE CLOTHES WE WORE - ANCESTORS

A large part of the family lived in China walk, Lambeth, which was at the Kennington end of the Lambeth Walk.

The family in this part of London, were the Brown's, they lived in the terraced houses of China Walk, most of which were destroyed during the bombing of London, since the end of the war I have lost contact with all of them, to my eternal regret.

Christmas was a time for a 'Booze up', there was nothing pious about anyone in our family during Christmas, or at anytime for that matter. It was time for jollification and a party,

A party in Lambeth was something special, especially at Christmas, the whole family gathered with rarely less than 20 adults and perhaps a dozen 'kids'. I clearly remember one such party when Christmas day was on a Monday. We went to the Browns on Friday evening, there was a crowd of children there, and we were all related in some way or other. As soon as we arrived all the men trooped off to the Kings Arms Pub', now the Lambeth Walk, this was the usual start to the party. They returned in a merry mood much later pushing a cart loaded with drinks of all kinds, plus a barrel of beer, drinks for the ladies, drinks for the children, and anything else that was considered essential for the party.

On Saturday night the fun started, Teddy Brown was wounded at Gallipoli in the First World War; he lost a leg during the landing, and walked very well on an artificial leg. For some reason he always removed his artificial leg before he played a trombone, which he played very well, I don't think it had anything to do with his musical talents. My mother was a good pianist, rather better than my father; there were times when they would sit down to the same keyboard for a duo. That was something to hear it always drew a lot of applause. An uncle played a piano accordion, and once all three got together it sounded well. As the night wore on discord would enter the music, but by that time no one noticed anyway.

I learned all the music hall songs, and was able to recognise many of the artiste's from their photographs on the music sheets. I have passed many of the songs on to my daughter, and now she in turn is passing them on to her children. I feel it is an important part of history that these cockney music hall songs should be remembered. Songs such as Gus Elen's 'My Old Dutch', G.H.Elliot's 'Lily of Laguna', Chirgwin, who was the 'White Eyed Kaffir' and Randolph Sutton's 'On Mother Kelly's Doorstep'. These are only a few that I knew when I was not even 12 years old. It is a richness of life that we should retain forever.

    I am digressing. The Christmas party was a 3-day jollification; you slept when you were tired in any place you found comfortable or convenient, father had bought a new suit for this party, he and two others decided to sleep on top of a table. Sleep was not forthcoming as

Lambeth Walk

one or another kept falling off, to solve the problem the table was turned upside down, they laid inside and slept well. Came the morning, and father found a huge rent in the back of his trousers, nails protruding through the tabletop had caused this, the table was many years old. Father received the length of mother's tongue when she found out. I can only assume that because of the three of them being so inebriated they didn't feel the nails sticking in them. For the rest of the time we stayed there father slept in his long johns, for most of Boxing day he walked around in that state because some had taken his trousers away to see if they could be repaired, they reappeared during the evening.

Father was always the fool, always acting, always dancing, he was very light on his feet, and in his younger days he was a good tap dancer, and could do funny walks in the shade of Max Wall. When he was sober he was very talented, and always in demand for his party pieces, when he was the worse for drink he was silly and pathetic. His big fault was that he could not resist a pretty face, and that led him to making a nuisance of himself to the lady concerned. There were many rows between him and my mother due to his lady chasing, and more than once she caught him in compromising situations, in some strange way she found great satisfaction in breaking up his assignations, he was always complaining that he didn't have much fun.

Father was born at 202 Weedington Road, Camden Town, North-West London, on the 3rd of February 1891 and was Christened Henry Edward. He married my mother on the 28th of April 1924, they both married from 1 Strathleven Road, Brixton, South West London.

My Grand-father Bannister was a handsom cab driver who was killed at the age of 42 while drunk, it is sorrowful that my direct paternal forbears deaths were the result of excessive drinking, but not I. It is giving me much pleasure revising this story at the age of 77. Grandfather was a very heavy drinker, I have had the following tale related to me many times. He always came home drunk, sitting on top of his cab, when he left his usual Pub' his cronies would heave him up to the seat at the rear of the cab, then his horse would take him home without any guidance, a journey of about 2 miles. The entrance to the stable yard was through a low arch beneath the house next door, this arch led to a large open area at the back of Weedington Road, this area contained a large number of stables and sheds which were occupied by various cab and horse proprietors. On arriving at the arch the horse would stop just as grandfather was to smash his head onto the top of the arch. Aunt Mary would see him lolling in the cab seat and would cross the road and drag him down, take him indoors and put him to bed. The horse would then walk on of it's own accord into the yard where the yard boys would unharness it and stable the horse and put the cab away. This was a daily ritual.

Father was a great imbiber of Guinness and followed his father's habits; he worked up to the First World War in the printing trade, as did my mother. He volunteered for the army in 1915 and joined the London Irish Rifles, he was posted to various places, but because he wanted to go to France he deserted, he then rejoined the Royal Welch Fusiliers. It soon became apparent that he had received army training, he was court martialled and was sentenced to be posted immediately to France, exactly as he wanted.

He fought in the 2nd battle of Ypres and was severely wounded. This is his story as recounted during a sober moment. "We went over the top, and a German machine gun in a pill box was causing heavy casualties, my mate Bill and I were ordered to silence the machine gun. I left the shell hole we were in and ran forward, Bill was wounded and knocked out, and I made it to the pillbox. As I put a hand grenade through the slit where the machine gun barrel was the entire box exploded in pieces. I remember seeing my mates advancing pass me, I half laid in a shell hole full of mud, I thought my left arm was severed as I could not see or feel it, all I seemed to do was sleep, later I was picked up by some of our boys. I was put in an ambulance and I passed out again. The ambulance held eight stretchers, four on top and four on the floor, I was put on the floor.

I remember a terrible ride back to the base hospital, at the base there was a procedure that the wounded were taken straight in for examination, and the dead were left at the side of the road for burial. As the orderlies unloaded us I heard one of them say, "leave him here he is a goner, he is covered in blood", I shouted out, no I am not, the blood is from the poor sod above me, it had been dribbling over me during the journey back".

He was told afterwards that as he put the grenade through the slit in the pillbox, one of our own shells blew the box to pieces. Bill was killed, and father was badly wounded, he laid in the shell hole for three days and was picked up by our soldiers as they retreated from their advance.

How did they know that it was one of our own shells that blew the box up? Fathers wound was caused by a piece of shrapnel; it had passed through his shoulder from the front, and had shattered his shoulder blade out at the rear. A piece of nose cap was taken from his wound, and the numerals stamped on it identified it as a British 5" Howitzer shell. Father had this piece for many years; it was lost when our home was bombed in 1941.

His wound needed dressing every week until it finally healed in 1928. The year I was born he was advised to have the arm amputated, he steadfastly refused and was later able to use the arm with some restriction, but was never able to raise the arm above shoulder height.

He often claimed that he had been recommended for the Military Medal for bravery in the face of the enemy, the family dismissed it as 'one of fathers tales', however, when he was working one night as the commissioner at the front of the Lyric Theatre in London he was approached by a stranger who asked could they meet for a quick drink during the interval, father agreed. When they met the stranger introduced himself as fathers Company Commander in 1916, he was a Captain. He had recognised father and had a story to tell him. This is the tale, the Battalion Commander had recommended him for the MM on the report that the Captain had made of his attack on the pillbox, any recommended awards had to be signed by the senior officer of the day of the occasion, the appropriate papers were made out to be signed but unfortunately the Major himself was killed during another attack against the enemy on the day that father entered hospital. I remember some correspondence between father, the Captain and the War Office, all to no avail.

He was determined to keep his arm as mobile as possible, he often said, "You never know, I may be needed in the next war", he was, but in a different capacity. When his wound healed he was left with a hole very nearly through his shoulder, I remember putting a finger in the hole in the front, and another finger in the hole at the back, and although I could not touch fingers , I could feel them.

Gruesome? I suppose so, but there, he was my father, and he was one of the lucky ones to return home alive from the carnage that was Ypres.

Father was, ever since I could remember, a heavy drinker, during my younger days there were constant rows between my parents over his flirting with other women, even when in my mothers company. He gambled a lot on Dog racing, he was vain, impeccable in his dress, constantly getting himself into trouble, with my mother constantly getting him out again, he was a gigantic sprucer, always telling stories that were not true, then he would try to lie his way out of them. He was a great boaster, and would take on more than he could cope with, or even understand. He was very selfish in his ways, making sure that mother always came second to his wishes.

When war broke out in 1939 father gave up his job with W.H.Smith & Son Ltd, and took a job with J.Lyons & Co Ltd, at the Brixton depot where I was serving my apprenticeship. He was employed there as a van cleaner, and at that time it was company policy to wash all of the 30 vans each day, he was one of a team of three men.

At the onset of the air raids during the war, a compulsory government order was made that all business premises would have a full time paid fire watcher at night. Father was offered this job at Lyons and readily accepted, he said he felt that he could at last play his part in the war once more. He performed his job with valour, but all his efforts on the night of the fire could not stop the depot burning.

After the depot in Brixton was closed he found another job with the Lyric Theatre in London; he was the Senior Commissioner. Once more he was back in uniform, he remained in this job until he was 86, and was then forcibly retired, he was very active and fit, his eyes gave him a little trouble as did his finger nails, but this was a legacy of meeting with mustard gas during the first world war.

After he finally gave up work he lived in Brixton until the death of my mother. He then moved to Leatherhead to live with my wife and I. He was very unhappy there away from his pub' pals, and after he contracted pneumonia and because of alcohol withdrawal symptoms his mind gave way. He almost becoming an imbecile, he talked gibberish and acted very strangely. After a while he was admitted to Epsom General Hospital, where he remained for a year in the Psychiatric Ward. He amazingly recovered from the pathetic being that he had become. The Royal British Legion offered him a home at Broadstairs which he readily accepted, he was at last home among his own generation. Here he was able to sit and talk of the First World War all day with the other 'Old Soldiers' at the Home.

He survived until he was 93, heavily imbibing Guinness until the end, he even left £50 for the inmates to have a merry drink after his funeral.

An Apprenticeship to Life

His funeral was the largest the home had ever had, two coaches of inmates attended, the Union Jack was draped over his coffin, the Legion Standard was lowered, and the 'Last Post' was sounded, he was then cremated. I can imagine his last thoughts, he would have said "I enjoyed it all, to hell with the rest of them", He was truly Rudyard Kipling's 'Tommy'.

About three years before he died, I discovered that he was eligible for the Defence Medal having been a full time firewatcher for three years during the war. I applied for it on his behalf, and it was sent to him. He was very proud of it, as he was with his First World War medals. These are now framed and hung in my home alongside with my own and other family member's medals.

He had vivid memories of the First World War, my lasting regret is that I had not recorded them, being an undergraduate at Canterbury University reading history I should have known better. Very soon now, possibly during the next five years, there will be no one alive who will be able to give a first hand account of being a soldier in the First World War. We seem to know more about life under the Romans than we do of life under King George V.

Mother was born in Cornwall Road, Lambeth, and was Christened Ethel Maude Rogers, the family moved to Choumont Road, Peckham for a while and then moved to Strathleven Road, Brixton. Mother spent most of her working life in the printing industry, her work was mostly on sewing or stapling machines putting magazines together, at one time Aunt Win and mother worked together at a firm called Kit-Kat,(Not the chocolate bar).

My parents married in 1924, from Strathleven Road, mother in her teens gained a name for chasing Boys, and like father she liked her tipple, which then was always Port wine.

They met when they both worked at Odham's press, in 1919. Father had just started work after his wound convalescence and was still handicapped to a great extent. A certain manager constantly gave him the heavy work which he could not manage, mother felt sorry for him and took up the cudgel on his behalf, she had a row with the manager who promptly sacked both of them, they found other work and started courting.

I was born a year after they were married, and five years after me came my brother Leslie Edward after I was born mother did no other work other than as a housewife.

After World War Two, about 1950, she started work again as a cleaner/ticket collector at the Apollo theatre, almost next door to father at that time, she eventually moved to the Lyric and retired at the age of 80.

Mother's life was one of keeping an eye on father as he got drunk each night before she became in the same condition, I well remember as a child that mother was a clean and tidy person. In later years things drifted as drink took a hold of her and her nights became relegated to sleeping in an arm chair, her bed was never slept in, she and her sister Winifred were great drinking pals, at mid-day as well as mid-night, yet they seldom drank at home.

Mothers death was partly due to fathers selfishness, she had become partially crippled and walked with two sticks, one very cold winter night he insisted that she should accompany him to their 'Local', a walk of just over a mile. They returned home in their usual inebriated state, to their Council flat. Mother contracted pneumonia, the next evening, and ill as she was, father again insisted she went out with him, she went and never recovered. She simply went home, sat in her chair and died fully clothed.

Her funeral was a traditional one peculiar to pub' life, which I related to in the previous chapter, and yet of all the hundreds of pub' friends she had made during her lifetime none were at her funeral and only 4 relatives paid their last respects.

When she went a little of Acre Lane went with her, she had been using two pubs' that were opposite each other for over 65 years. She was one of the originals of whom there were only a handful left then, there are probably none left today.

She had a rich singing voice, and could play the piano quite well, always the centre of the party, and could be relied upon to 'Whack the old Joanna all night', in the pub' the cry was often heard" Come on Ethel, giv'us a song". Her favourite song was 'She is the Belle of New York', this was the theme song from a long running musical at the turn of the century.

She was never a good cook, I can only remember plain simple food, and during the last 10 years of her life she existed on soups and bread and cheese. No amount of persuasion would induce her to eat anything else, yet she survived; there is no doubt that the large amount of Guinness she drank accounted for her stamina.

Mother never went out without a hat on her head, she considered it improper not to do so; she was never known to entertain at home. During the last 20 years of her life, when I visited her, I would only be in her flat for a few minutes when she would say, "Come on boy lets go and have a drink".

She was never envious of anyone or anything, but when she had drunk too much she had a vicious and spiteful temper. She would never forgive a spite against her, if it was against father it didn't matter, then he was a fool for taking umbrage.

I never knew her to have a liking for pets, towards animals she was really cold, and of course they didn't fit in with Pub' life. Her relations with relatives were to put it bluntly, fiery, she was always having rows with her sisters, and my Aunt Julie would have nothing to do with her at all. My Uncle Jim, her elder brother was placid and tolerant toward her, but then he was away from home a lot with his work. She was always in debt, and I was often answering the door to debt collectors to tell them, "Sorry mum's not in".

Mother was not without courage, and would fiercely defend that which was hers.

About 1936, in the Acre Lane area there was a spate of attempted interference's against small boys by a tall middle aged man. It was reported in the local papers, and one day while waiting outside the 'Duke of Wellington' I went to the pub toilet which was up an alleyway at the side of the pub. Inside I was accosted by this man, I ran outside and called my father, but it was my mother who went inside the toilet and dragged the man out, he had the marks of her handbag on his face. Men from the pub' held him until Police arrived. He was eventually found guilty of many charges of indecency and one of grievous harm to one poor boy, mother was commended by the judge at the mans trial.

My brother was Leslie Edward, He was tragically killed when he was five and a half years old, Les was as fair as I was dark. He had a mass of blond hair and bright blue eyes, he was an effeminate boy with a loving way, he was mother and father's favourite whereas I was Aunt win and Uncle Jim's favourite. I cannot remember much of my brother, being only ten years old I had lots of boyish things on my mind other than a brother, he had few naughty habits, and yet it was a naughty act that killed him. I have only one photograph of him with me, I cannot reconcile him to that 'photo, but I accept that it is a picture of my brother Leslie, my only sibling.

He died so tragically, he had started school only a week before he was killed, the first week he had been taken to school by my mother. The second week I was told to take him, the school was the Sudbourne Road, LCC Junior, just off Brixton Hill. I had strict instructions to hold his hand when we were nearing the very busy Acre Lane, when we were nearing the 'Lane' I told him to hold my hand. He laughed and ran out into the road as a Taxi was nearly passing, the Taxi hit him. I remember a terrible thud and saw a shoe thrown high in the air; he lay very still in the roadway. I took to my heels and ran straight home and told mother. By the time mother arrived at the accident the ambulance had arrived, she went off in the ambulance to the hospital.

Leslie died six hours later, had he lived he would have been crippled for life in speech and hearing, it was a merciful relief from his short life.

Ever after that day mother blamed me for his death, even now I recall the look she gave me whenever Leslie was mentioned, I was utterly bewildered as to why I was to blame. I had bad dreams for weeks afterwards. Even as I retype this script, 67 years afterwards, it hurts to remember it all over again.

I was taken to the inquest, I remember the coroner saying to me, "Do you know where little boys go to if they tell the truth?" I said, "Yes sir", he replied "If you want to go to heaven you must tell the truth". I answered all of his questions as best as I could. He ended by saying to my parents, "It was wrong of both of you to trust a ten year old boy to be responsible for a much younger child".

From that day there was a much-changed attitude toward me by my mother that lasted until she died, her intake of alcohol increased greatly from that time. I believe to this day that Leslie's death broke her somewhat and she never really recovered. There was an air of gloom over the family for years afterwards, even during family arguments, up to my late teens, Leslie's name would be mentioned as though he had been killed deliberately. He is buried in Lambeth cemetery, despite the loss to my mother she only visited his grave once, on the first anniversary of his death. This was another strange aspect of my mother's make-up.

Aunt Win (Winifred Rogers), was a generous person with a warm personality, her younger life was full of men friends, and yet she never married. She was not endowed with good looks, she made up for the lack of beauty with her popularity, she always wore a diaphanous dresses and edge to edge coats which were fashionable in the 30's.

In later years she had a male friend whom I knew as Jo-Jo, I never knew his real name, they were devoted lovers for many years, Jo-Jo was married, his wife would not give him a divorce, therefore Aunt Win and Jo-Jo were everything to each other except as man and wife. Jo-Jo had a daughter, and when he died he left everything to her and not a penny to Aunt Win, she was broken, and she had given so much of her life to him, and had lost all.

She eventually moved to a flat in Dalyell Road, Stockwell, on then to a single room, she died at the age of 92, with all her faculties working right to the end of her days.

Uncle Jim (James Robert Rogers), now, here in my eyes was a man among men, as a child I worshipped him, I saw in him a Rudyard Kipling, a man of learning, a man of patriotism, a man who firmly believed in the traditional way of English life. He had a command of English that was the equal of H.V.Morton, with all of Mortons understanding of the common man. I have tried all of my life to emulate James Robert, and looked upon him as my spiritual father, I spent many happy hours in his company just watching him painting and constructing wireless sets in the early days of 'London 2LO'. He once wrote a book based on his reminiscences of theatre life, he wrote it just for the joy of writing, he had it typewritten and bound, and no one could persuade him to send it to a publisher for their perusal. I tried to read it when I was young but it was beyond my comprehension. The book was believed to have been destroyed in the bombing of Ellerslie Square in 1941. He worked all his life in the theatre world, he worked on many famous shows, and during his later years he toured with the 'Fol de Rols', and there were few seaside piers that he had not worked in. His job was that of a stage designer and carpenter. For a great number of years before WW2 he had a lady friend, there was no romance, just good friend ship. My mother and father always spoke of her with respect, I cannot remember her name, she was a white haired gracious person, someone once said that she had a title of some sort, I suppose it could have been true. She originally lived in a large house near Kings Lynn in Norfolk, and later moved to Crystal Palace in Southeast London.

Uncle Jim over the years constructed many toys for me of all descriptions, the last one he built was for my eleventh Christmas, this was a railway layout on a large scenic baseboard, about 6'x 8', this gave me many hours of pleasure, and was eventually destroyed when our house was bombed in 1941.

He was a great smoker, and always had a smokers cough; his cigarettes were W.D. & H.O. Wills 'Goldflakes', one of the more expensive cigarettes in the pre WW2 years. I had never known him not to have a prolonged cough first thing in the morning, it was a comfort to me just to hear it, he was away from home at times when he was touring with Binnie Hale's company, she was a well known actress in the 30's.

I missed him greatly when he was away.

He was a prolific landscape painter, family gossip had it that he had a picture hung in the Royal Academy and that he was a member, this was never substantiated, I have two of his earlier paintings c.1924. I wish now that I had a photograph of him, often in life the things we cherish we didn't bother to keep.

During 1940/41 when an air raid warning was on, the Sunlight Laundry Ltd allowed the inhabitants of Ellerslie Square to use their shelters, which were situated in a field at the back of the laundry, it was during these nights that Uncle Jim started courting a much younger lady started by their meetings in the shelters, they were actually next door neighbours. Nell married him when he was 70, they had a son when he was 72, and he died, a victim of the Great Smog in 1962, when he was 89. Despite all warnings from the Government to elderly people to stay indoors and to keep out of the smog, he insisted on collecting his own old age pension and died of Pneumonia.

I was very sorrowful at his death and regret to this day that I did not know him so well in my adult life as I did as a child, nevertheless I have only the fondest memories of Jimmy Rogers.

Grandmother Rogers (Winifred). I never knew her, as she died only 4 months before I was born. I was told she was a kindly person, always dressed in black widows weeds which she wore since grandfather died. Her death was tragic, she was crossing Brixton High Street, from the 'Bon Marché' departmental store to 'Woolworth's' on the opposite side, as she passed behind a heavy horse drawn cart the tail board fell down onto her head. She was taken to hospital and never recovered. One event she was looking forward to was the birth of another grandchild, myself, it is said that the last words she uttered in hospital was to my mother, and they were, "Look after the babe", I was born just thirteen weeks later.

Grandfather Rogers (Fredrick) died long before I was born, I know little of him, except that he died of prolonged inhalation of wood and ivory dust. He was a self employed turner, he had his own lathe set up in a small shed in the back garden of our home in Strathleven Road, Brixton. The shed was still there when we moved away just before WW2. He worked as a contractor to Maples Ltd of Tottenham Court Road; he produced small wooden ornaments and ivory chess pieces to Maple's designs. Over the years there was little ventilation in the shed and the dust took its toll, he was only 45 years old when he died, such a young age with so much talent untapped

It is to my eternal regret that of all my grand parents, I knew only of my maternal grandmother. I firmly believe that in ones childhood years grandparents are so important, the invaluable experience of life that they have gone through should be the background of each childs growing years. The grandparents have the time and patience to teach this, ironically more time than the parents who are too busy raising a family.

My oldest aunt (Grace) Bertha Rogers married Albert French. She was born on the 9th of June 1883 at 12b Peabody Buildings, in the London Parish of StGiles, although their backgrounds were very similar to the rest of my family, they were always rather aloof and considered themselves a 'cut' above the others, certainly their home and furniture bore this out.

Uncle Albert, always Albert and never Bert, worked in the printing business as a compositor, a very well paid job. He was much better off than my father because of his job and also because he drank a lot less than my father and because of that he had a much better standard of living. He was able to buy his own home in Streatham, South London, then, as indeed even now, a select area. For about a year after my brother died we visited Aunt grace a lot, as usual we met in a pub', the 'Telegraph' at the top of Brixton Hill near the Prison. After they came out we always walked to their house and stayed for a while, without exception there was always a parcel of comics waiting for me, Uncle Albert brought them home for me from his work. The parcels contained around two dozen, a mixture of 'Tiger', 'Comic Cuts', 'Wizard',

'Adventure', 'Boys Own', 'Film Fun', 'Hotspur', and many others. They had no children of their own, whenever we met I was fussed and spoilt by them, to me, Aunt Grace seemed so old, she tended to dress in an Edwardian manner, but she was always very gracious in her deportment.

Following the usual family pattern we somehow lost touch with aunt Grace and Uncle Albert, in fact we were unaware that he had died. I found out many years later that she was living at Esher in Surrey, the Police notified mother that Aunt Grace had died, mother was next of kin but would have nothing to do with the probate and funeral arrangements. It fell to me to sort it out, I think Aunt Grace was the first one to die in the family and leave enough money to pay for the burial. As usual the vultures had been to work and had removed most of her possessions before I could make an inventory, the old peoples home where she had been living claimed a sum owing to them, and so the bulk of it went to them.

THE CLOTHES WE WORE

Children in Pre-WW2 wore clothes that one had to grow to make them fit, this was the accepted criteria when clothes were bought. I remember short trousers that reached the tops of my long socks, jackets that were too long in length and sleeves, the sleeves were turned up and worn until they looked too short, and then they were turned down again. The same treatment was given to short trousers, with these I wore a belt, not to hold them up, but to hold them in. I was never sure if I wore short long'uns or long short'uns. The belts I wore were made of elasticised material, and were adjustable by means of a sliding clip, a hook in the shape of a snake coupled the buckle with a head and a tail cast on it. They vanished from the markets towards the end of the war, but amazingly in the 21st century they are back on the markets again, entirely unchanged. This design has spanned at least 70 years.

Mother had a queer notion that braces as well as the belt should be worn; however the braces should not be seen. The problem was to connect the braces to the trousers whilst wearing them under a shirt that was tucked in the trousers. Mother's solution was to cut slits in the shirt pull the tabs of the braces through the slits and button them to the trousers. It looked, putting it mildly, rather weird, to my friends it was a source of never ending merriment. I was the only boy in the whole wide world who had his trousers held up in that fashion.

An Apprenticeship to Life

The shirts I wore were made of a heavy flannel material they were in any colour as long as they were grey, the material was thick enough to have been used as sail cloth, it was so itchy. Another garment was the Jersey, (see front cover picture) this was even itchier than the shirt, and this again was always grey with a striped tie, always striped in red, not down the tie but across. The long sleeves were a nuisance because of the trouble they caused when putting on a topcoat; mother was always struggling up my sleeves to pull the jersey sleeves down because they had gone up under my armpits. As usual the jerseys were bought far too large in order to 'Grow into it'. I always thought this 'Grow into it ' policy was an attitude of mind, as by the time one grew into and it fitted, it was worn out and had to be started all over again.

Shoes were always bought a size too large, and one thing I could never do, even to this day, was to tie a decent bow in a shoelace, my bows ended in double knots. I could never undo these when the shoe was on my foot, I was always told to undo the lace before taking the shoe off. I seldom wore the soles out, but oh how the uppers suffered.

Mother took out 'Provident 'cheques to buy our clothes, and always went to the shops in Brixton market that displayed the 'Provident' sign. I was told never to tell anyone that we bought 'On the Provident; more often than not the Provident man was chasing for payment, we were always in arrears. The only time mother paid up was when she wanted another cheque, I was often told to answer a knock on the door to tell the tally man that "Mum is out, can you come back next week?" Our rent was collected once a fortnight, and when the rent was paid someone else had a non-payment entry to make in their books, the object of this exercise was to ensure that there was money for the pub, and so the Tallymen were frustrated for their dues.

Father had a good blue Melton overcoat and a good suit, he only wore them for funerals and like activities, the clothing spent most of it's time in 'Uncles', the pawn shop, mother went in once a week to pay the interest on the loan.

In 1936 King George V died and was lying in state in Westminster Hall. We all went to see the catafalque, mother and father, Uncle Jim, Aunt Win', and I, it was a typical cold, wet, London day, steadily raining, and the queue took two hours to reach the Hall. We all were soaked, and fathers suit shrunk and never recovered from that outing and mother lost the source of another loan from 'Uncles'.

At 10 years old, to me, the laying in state was awe inspiring, there was a guard in full dress uniform at each corner, with the point of his sword resting on the toe cap of his boot, their hands rested on the hilt of the swords, and the guards were motionless.

The King lay in state in Westminster Hall just as his father; King Edward VII did in 1910. Westminster Hall is the largest Hall in England with an unsupported roof; it is 238ft long, 68ft wide and 90ft high. With the King at rest in the centre of the Hall it was Historic England at it's best.

Originally built by William Rufus, the massive roof was added by Richard II, and made from oak from Sussex, rotting timbers were replaced in 1923 by oaks from the same area in Wadhurst.

It is a hall of the famous and the infamous, including the trial of Charles I, the Proclamation of Cromwell, and trials of William Wallace, Sir Thomas Moore, and Earl of Sussex and Guy Fawkes.

It was the scene of the Kings champion riding fully armoured, for the last time in history into the Hall, at the coronation of George IV.

The people who died in the R.101 Airship disaster in 1930 were laid to rest here, the Hall suffered damage to the roof during WW2 when an oil bomb fell on the roof, again Wadhurst timber was used for the repairs.

The Hall has probably seen more English history than any other building, and was part of the old Palace of Westminster; to me as a child it was All England. We filed slowly past the catafalque, then out of the door at the far end, many, many thousands paid homage to their King during the three days it was opened, I wondered what it was all about, I know now, and I feel very privileged that I was there to be forming a tiny piece of history.

Father was a monarchist and a true Tory at heart, he could not abide the trade union movement, and yet he was at one time the representative for the Printers Chapel at Stamford Street, I once heard him confide to Uncle Jim that being Father Chapel was better than working.

Father always sought the easy way out of work, sometimes he even worked hard at avoiding work, invariably his antics increased the workload of others, and no one to this day has ever had more varied excuses for not being where he should be during his working day. When he was on night work, he would sleep under the printing presses; his colleagues told mother that it was a job to wake him up, even with the thunderous noise all around him. I visited the pressroom once, the noise was terrible.

He would never wear overalls; he would rather mess his good clothes up than protect them, overalls to him seemed to lower his standard of living. He always considered himself a cut above the rest, his mode of dress reflected his thoughts, he was always smart, always wore a tie, and for many years he refused to wear shirts with collars attached, he thought they were not the dress of a gentleman.

Winter or summer he wore a Trilby hat, and was never without a handkerchief in his top pocket, in fact his work mates called him 'The Toff'. He had a fad with shoes, they were always patent leather, and he would never have a hole in the sole, it was common in the thirties for people to have holes in the soles of their shoes. He mended all the family shoes, new soles and heels and the odd bits of stitching. Once a week all shoes were inspected and cleaned, and the cleaning was done with true spit.

I learned to repair shoes from him, and carried on the tradition until the mid 60's , after which my fortunes allowed me to send them for repair, shoes last much longer now, and do not need much repair, if indeed they can be repaired. I bought a pair of soft suede shoes from a stall in Merano, Northern Italy, the year was 1970, I still wear them, they are as soft as slippers, and the heels were repaired last year. They cost me 9000 Lira, then £3, They are 33 years old and still good.

I often went with father to Brixton market, there was a good leather stall there, he would bargain for a good piece and come away with enough to repair half a dozen pairs of soles, he knew his leather and would only buy best English hide, and it had to be stamped as such.

Most of our clothes were shop bought, mother was never one for sewing or knitting although she was a very good at darning socks. I remember being very good with socks; I seldom wore a hole in them. I always had knee length hose, the type that had turn over tops with a couple of coloured stripes, green, yellow, red or blue, according to whatever house you belonged to at school. As the socks were forever falling down there was an elastic garter underneath the tops. Socks were wonderful placed to keep things in, conkers, pieces of string, cigarette cards, bus tickets, all sorts of things were pushed down into safe keeping.

ANCESTORS

Grandfather was the first Bannister to migrate from the Shoreditch Parish of London. His ancestors have been traced back as far as 1750, all living within a few streets of each other in the same parish. At one time in Dukes Court, now underneath Trafalgar Square.

The occupations of various generations have included, Ostler, Cabman, and Silk Weaver, probably the Silk Weaver was employed by the last decendants of the Huguenot's who founded the industry in Shoreditch and Whitechapel Parishes of London, then Middlesex. Silkweaver Bannister worked as such for over 40 years and finished his working life almost at the end of the Silkweaving industry demise during the 1880's.

During the research of both my wife's and my own family names, it became very clear that with each new name discovered on both sides, the families were nearing each other, by the 1880's they were only two streets apart, it would be nice to know if they knew of each other in those long gone days. What a wonderful thought if it were possible to be able to visit them, as they lived and worked.

I have been fortunate to find that there was very little movement of both families from London, but then people had to walk where ever they went, whether it was for work or domestic reasons. If a person changed their job it had to be within walking distance, otherwise it would mean a move of residence, Public transport, if it was available could not be afforded.

So, my wife and I are true Londoners, both bred of the area of the Cockney, that is between the East End and the City, from generation after generation of Londoners true and proud, and as this story unfolds, Londoners who helped to defend it during its greatest trial in all its history.

CHAPTER 4

HOUSES WE LIVED IN – THE NEIGHBOURHOODS

STREET VENDORS

HOUSES WE LIVED IN

The house I was born in was in a notorious slum area that encompassed streets from St Pancras Station to the border with Hampstead, Camden Town was a district of St Pancras. It is now in the Borough of Camden.

Weedington Road consisted of three storied terraced houses, the road was bisected by Queens Crescent, I lived in the northern half of the road which was more bug ridden than the southern half. The house was number 202, the last house on the right; there was an alley alongside the house which was entered through a pair of gates and passing under an archway. This led to a very large open space at the rear which contained many stables and stalls with harness stores, there was also coverage storage for Handsom cabs and traders carts.

Opposite the houses on the northern side was an 8 feet high brick wall, this was the wall at the end of the back yards of the houses opposite which faced on Ashdown Street. The Ashdown Street house which backed onto number 202 was the home of fathers sister, my Aunt Mary, at 37 Ashdown Street.

Aunt Mary was married to Charley Tasker, my two cousins were Florie and Reggie, both much older than I was, my only living grandparent lived with them, and she was my father's mother, Mary Bannister. The house they lived in was a two-story house occupied only by the Taskers, they were considered fortunate by the standards of those times.

On the three floors of 202 there lived five families, on the ground floor there lived three single persons, one to each of the three rooms, on the first floor all three rooms were occupied by a family of four, on the top floor we had the two rooms. There was a kitchen at the rear, heated by a large kitchen range, this was our normal living room, divided by a landing was the front room which was the largest room in the house. This room was the bedroom where all four of us slept, it had two sash windows that looked out on to Weedington Road. Mother and father had a double bed across the right hand window, on this bed I, my brother Leslie and my father were born. I slept in a large hospital type bed with lift up sides, after Leslie was born, he slept at one end and I at the other. When mother and father performed their marital functions, the side of my bed was lifted and a blanket draped over the side to black me out. Although at that early age I didn't understand what was going on, I quickly learned all the different noises that emitted from their corner, depending of course the state of father's inebriation.

All our eating was done in the kitchen, we had our baths in the kitchen, it was our living room, our playroom, and when we were young it was our world.

Water was drawn from a tap and sink on the landing below ours, we drew every drop of water from there, and all our waste water had to be poured away down the sink, I remember mother carrying the waste water away by the pailful, to the sink downstairs after we had had a bath. Father in his usual inebriated state, once tried to carry the bath of water down the stairs to empty it, and succeeded quite ably in tipping the contents down stairs. Naturally our neighbour below us did not take kindly to a large gush of water flowing in under her door, and once more there was a neighbourly row.

We were one of the few dwellers that had covering on the stairs, of course in those days if anyone had floor covering of any kind you were considered to be doing well. This was due to one of fathers acquisitions, He had heard that a house had become vacant further down the street, together with a friend, late one night, they visited the house and stripped the covering from the stairs and shared it between them. Behold, the next day we had stair covering, well really it was Congoleum, a form of printed roofing felt. He even laid some on the stairs below the poor lady who had the water poured under her door, a strange way of making peace.

The lavatory was down four flights of stairs, out into the back yard and at the end of the path to the back gate. Mother kept a pail with a lid on it on our landing which she emptied from time to time. It was a long haul to the lavatory with a slopping pail.

Cooking was done on the kitchen range and oven, coal was 11½d a cwt', on our landing there was a coal bin which held 2 cwt'. The coalman would not carry the coal up the stairs, he simply tipped the coal onto the path, when I came home from school it was my job to guard the coal until dad came home, otherwise neighbours below us would 'nick' a pail or two. Mind you father was up to it with their coal just as much they were up to it with ours. When father arrived home he would empty the slop pail and then carry the coal up the four flights until all was in the bin. When the job was done he was tired indeed, but not too tired to go to the pub' after he had had his tea.

The kitchen was warm, but sadly, although father always had enough money to go to the pub' there were times when he would not keep the coal bin full, and of course we were cold. During winter the bugs were not very active but in the summer at night it was sheer hell, the hotter it became the more the bugs went on the rampage. Most of the adults sat out in the streets talking into the small hours rather than face the bugs in bed.

There was no interior decorating carried out, paint peeled and wood rotted, any decorating done inside was at the tenants expense. The outside had never been renovated since the houses were built in the 1880's. father had only repapered the bedroom once, but because the job lot of cheap paper had not been enough there was a gap where the old paper could be seen. I laid in my bed many a night trying to work out if the pattern would have matched if he had had enough to complete the job.

As children we played in the street, there were few cars about, mostly the odd police car and the Doctors vehicle, traders had either handbarrows or horse drawn carts. A couple of times a week after school, we would go down to Queen's Crescent where there was a long street market, we would search about under the fruit and veg' stalls and take home a box of bruised and half rotted fruit, mother would cut away the bad pieces, and after it was washed it was wholesome, I probably ate more fruit then than I ever do today.

The front of the house had a small garden, is was really a dirt patch, I was forbidden to play there for reasons which I have mentioned in Chapter 1. There were a goodly number of children living in the house, we all got on together very well, more so than our parents did at times. Whenever there was a fall out between the adults I was told not to play with their children and of course they were told not to play with me, but we children were a mind above petty quarrels and ignored it all.

Food quickly went bad, as it would in times long before refrigeration, we had a meat 'safe' hung on the wall outside the kitchen window. This was a large box with a door; the two sides and the door were open, but covered with wire mesh. Fresh meat was placed in the safe, this keeps flies and other insects away, and as the walls between the houses never had sunshine on them it was a cool storage area. I had always known the box to be rickety. One day the inevitable happened, the bottom dropped out and good food disappeared three stories down and crashed into the yard much to the delight of the hoard of stray cats that came from the stables at the back of the houses. The repair of the box was a strange affair. Because it needed a 30ft ladder to reach the location and there was no such thing available, father had a bright idea such as he often had, he took the window frame out, removed a pane of glass and mounted a box in place of the glass, this was great in the summer but as soon as the winter came it let in the cold air. Great man my dad for good ideas that always seemed to go wrong.

Mother had a fad for fly papers in the summer, I remember staring for hours at flies in their last throes stuck on a paper, until one day I somehow became entangled with a fly paper across my head, now fly paper glue is impervious to soap, and no amount of washing would remove the glue, I ended up with my hair being washed in paraffin.

I formed an opinion that because these papers had a prefix, fly, the flies came in their dozens to have a look at them. That is why rooms without papers have less flies than rooms that have them, I think this is called someones law.

Now came time to move house, Uncle Jim had the lease of a good house, number 1, Strathleven Road, Brixton, London, S.W.4. William Booth described this road as being occupied by 'Fairly comfortable families

An Apprenticeship to Life

with good ordinary earnings'. His upstairs tenants had moved away and so he offered the flat to my father.

It was a busy road, often used as a short cut between Acre Lane and Brixton Hill; the houses were all in a good state of repair. We were in the first house around the corner from Acre lane. On the corner was a greengrocers owned by an English naturalised Italian born man named Tunesi, he had a horse that was stabled the other side of our hall wall, often we would hear the horse kick the wall during the night. Neighbours next door were kindly people; far removed from the strident people we had left behind in the slums.

We had a clean start, all our furniture and clothing was fumigated before we left Camden Town and a lot of the old furniture was left behind. One of the main benefits was that father had a much easier and quicker journey to work We had three rooms, this was a 33% improvement. There was a small scullery off the kitchen which mother used for cooking, in fact mother used it as a small kitchen, there was a gas cooker there as well as our own water tap and a sink. the toilet was at the rear of the down stairs kitchen but because there was a door connecting the passageway to the garden there was no need to disturb any one. The toilet was in it's own enclosure in the garden. The garden was well kept by Uncle Jim and was almost as it was when he had taken over the tenancy after my Grandfather died tragically; this is described in a later chapter.

At the end of the garden there was a gate let into the rear garden wall, this led into an overgrown alleyway of which we were at the end, turning right, the alley passed the back of about ten houses, then turned sharp left and led out to a passage between two houses in Branksome Road. This was directly opposite the spot where my brother Leslie was killed, I will return to his story later.

Uncle Jim thought it would be a good idea if he and my father cleared the alley at the back as this would be a short cut to school and would save walking along the very busy Acre Lane in due course the gate was freed and a new bolt was fitted. Neighbours were warned and on one Sunday morning there was a group of men slashing and clearing the alley. A horse and cart from the council took the rubbish away and slowly householders began to use the shortcut to the shops, as house owners probably did when the houses were first built.

Leslie and I only used the back way a few times, it ceased almost as quickly as it began, here is the reason why. Uncle Jim was often away for a few days due to his work, he came home at all hours, often late at night. Soon after we began to use the alley it became time for him to be away again, he particularly asked father to make sure that the back gate was locked at night to prevent any intruders, he returned late one night and found the gate not only unlocked but ajar. There followed a heated argument which resulted in Uncle Jim locking the gate and that was the end of the short cut, this was a typical attitude of father's, if there was nothing of interest in anything for him, then he just didn't do it, such selfishness.

Our kitchen was a nice large room with an open fire; we really used it as a living room. We had the front upstairs room which was the largest room in the house, all four of us slept in the room, but now my brother and I had our own beds. The back room was Aunt Win's. She had her room on the top floor because the two ground floor front rooms were Uncle Jim's, the large one was his bedroom and the small one was his workroom. Here he did his paintings, built his wireless sets, stored his tools, and kept his trunks and cases. He was a stage carpenter and designer for the Fol-De-Rols, a famous concert party. In his spare time he was always making wireless sets, mother said he had one of the first sets in Lambeth. I remember when I was about 4 years old in 1929 having head phones put to my ears and hearing voices and music, and being scared.

Uncle Jim made a set for my parents, one with a large horn type loudspeaker, mother had many happy hours with it listening to Radio Luxembourg, there were many plays on during the evening, and of course my favourite was 'The Ovaltinees'. It kept father out of the pubs' for less than a week. Another good station was Radio Fecamp, there were lots of popular music, the station is still extant but has lost it's popularity.

The word radio didn't enter use until the WW2, before then it was always wireless, before the war year's most wireless sets were powered from batteries. Sets had two batteries, a dry 90volt one that was made from 60 cells wired together, and when it went flat it was thrown away and replaced. The much smaller of the batteries was a wet one, and was of lead acid construction. This could be purchased outright whereby the owner paid for it to be charged, or it could be hired for 6d (2½p) a week plus the same amount for charging.

An Apprenticeship to Life

The local battery charger was at Page Brothers in Acre lane, both brothers were elderly and also ran a car electrical repair garage at the rear of their shop. The shop had a display of car components laid out, and at the rear there was a large charging table which always had a least 12 batteries on charge, all bubbling away. As soon as one entered the shop there was noticed a strong smell of sulphuric acid.

About the age of 12 I worked for Page's for a considerable time, I was the battery delivery boy. Every Saturday morning I went to the shop and found my trolley loaded with charged batteries, I had a delivery book and a list of customers to visit, each battery had a ticket on it with the customer's name and address. I would tear off a half of the ticket and exchange it for 6d for charging plus 6d for rental, if it was the customers own battery it would be 6d for charging, most owners had two batteries. I usually managed to deliver 20 batteries in the four hours work. I did very well; I was paid 2/- by Page's and was usually paid a 2d tip by customer's, 5/- was a very good sum to have. The charge for the dry battery was according to make was 7/6d to 11s (37½p to 55p). I had this job until I started my apprentice when I was 14.

At quite an early age, Uncle Jim taught me how to use a small hand drill and do simple jobs using Bakelite. This is a brown semi-hard material; I have always believed this to be a milk by product as it smelled strongly of sour milk as it heated up when being drilled. Today of course better materials have replaced Bakelite. This period was a rich one of learning to grow up in; it was a time of pioneering and innovation. Also a time to learn as things evolved, to become a part of them because you helped to build them and make them work, not as today with pre-finished articles that are thrown away if they fail. A repair is impossible if it is not understood how things work. Skills are becoming lost, mainly due to the fact that there is now no incentive to learn when one is young, a child will only learn what is placed before it, and alas there is no incentive to be inquisitive to ask why and how. So, we must return to my story. The ground floor flat had electric light, whereas on the first floor we had gas lighting and cooking. All the rooms had double gas burners for the lighting; this made the rooms much brighter than we had in Camden Town. The gas mantle fascinated me, whenever father had to fit a new one there was a set procedure to follow. The mantle was made of woven cotton and was tied to a base made of porcelain, it looked like an upside down bag with a base about 1½" in dia', the base was fixed to the burner simply by giving it a half turn. Now came the part of my enjoyment, father struck a match and set the mantle alight, quite a fire really. The ash retained its shape and the secret was not to shake or bump it. If it was treated so, then it would simply collapse into a heap of dust, if all was right then a lighted match held near the mantle with the gas turned on resulted in a bright pale yellow light that burned with a noise between a hiss and a roar. The jet had to be removed to be cleaned, usually once a week, father could never do this when he returned from the pub', he had to do it before he went out.

One of my pleasures around this time was to read a copy of 'Meccano Magazine', they were usually old second hand ones, and I could not afford to buy the current monthly copy. However, around the corner in Acre Lane there was a small tobacco and confectioners shop run by two elderly sisters, the rear of their shop backed onto our garden, we always thought of them as being Posh or 'stuck up'. One morning Uncle Jim shouted up stairs that he had found a parcel in the garden for me. In the parcel was about a dozen copies of back numbers of 'Meccano Magazine', it transpired that the sisters had thrown them over the wall. Uncle Jim always bought his cigars and cigarettes from them and they had asked him if I would be interested in the books, they often visited a nephew who had hundreds of the books for disposal, and so every time they visited him they brought a fresh supply for me. This lasted for at least two years, until he was called up when war broke out. I never knew what happened to him, or what happened to the sisters, they retired and moved away from London in 1940.

Our bedroom, for the first time in our lives had a carpet on the floor, it was not new, Uncle Jim brought it home from a stage show, it was a square, about 9' x 9', I seemed to have spent hours following the snake patterns round the edge.

The bedroom looked out across Strathleven Road, opposite was a paled 6' high fence, this enclosed a yard belonging to Owen Bros.', Rolls-Royce agents, beyond that was an extensive nursery growing all kinds of foodstuffs. Set into the fence opposite our front door was a small cabin or kiosk where cigarettes and sweets were sold; this was owned by a tiny frail lady called Mrs Sutclift. We had a view across the yard to the side of a United Dairies shop, and each morning I would make a mark on the window level with the top of the new 150' chimney as the building of the new 'Sunlight Laundry' progressed. Later the yard was purchased and a new block of flats was built, 'Strathleven Court' blocked our nice view forever.

In 1936 the lease of 1 Strathleven Rd was nearly at an end, the new rent would rise sharply, Uncle Jim said it would be better to move on. So ended some of the happier years of my life, except for the one terrible incident of my brother's death which I related earlier.

Through one of fathers drinking pals' he heard of a vacant flat at 38 Ellerslie Square, Clapham. It was about ½ of a mile from our old house, this first floor flat was on a corner site and was a great improvement to Strathleven Road, the slum of Camden Town was now very far away indeed. We had a large front room which overlooked the Square, a back bedroom which also overlooked the Square, and above all we at last had our own lavatory which was a great blessing, we even had our own toilet roll, and paper on a string was but a memory. I must confess though I used to like trying to understand reading things on pieces of pink newspaper in the 'lav', I didn't know then that the newspaper was the 'Financial Times'. Father picked these up on the trams on his way home from work, and carrying one of these under one's arm gave the impression that one was something in the City. How we learned things in funny places.

My parents had the front room as their bed room and I had the back room, there was a small scullery off the kitchen which contained a small bath with a fitted flat top, a gas cooker, a gas hot water heater and a sink below the water heater. The kitchen was used as the sitting / dining room, it had an open fire and was very cosy in the winter. For the first time we had electric light, and we soon had a modern radio, although second hand.

The downstairs flat was occupied by a family named Tugwell, Mr Tugwell was the manager of a large furniture showroom on the corner of Acre Lane and Brixton Road opposite Lambeth Town Hall, the showrooms were called Collier's, probably the largest furniture company in South London in pre-war days. He was always very smartly dressed and kept very much to himself, as indeed did his wife. Their daughter Anne was a beautiful girl, a year older than myself and I was absolutely dotty over her. When I made my feelings known to her I was totally spurned, and took a long time to get over it. She never mixed with any of the girls and boys of the Square, yet when she was just 15 she was courted by a man much older than she was, I was told he was her uncle, uncle? Pull the other one.

One Sunday there was such a hullabaloo, my mother was rushing up and down the stairs with towels and buckets of hot water, and I could hear Mrs Tugwell screaming and crying. Father went off to the pub', and I asked what was the matter and was told it was a miscarriage. Once more I had to look in the dictionary to find out what it was, no one ever told me anything. Uncle Jim bought me books that I could learn from.

All my friends lived within 300 yards of number 38, and here in this house I spent three of the happiest years of my early teens.

Uncle Jim went to live at Sydenham, and Aunt Win went to live near another of my mother's sisters, Julie. Uncle Jim moved to our Square very soon after we moved there, and in 1941 two 500kg bombs, which experts said were chained together dropped neatly at the back of Uncle Jim's house. The resulting blast wiped out our Square completely, not one of the 52 houses was left habitable. Miraculously there were only minor injuries, and everyone who had a pet found them alive but scared. The Square was eventually rebuilt with prefabricated homes, and sometime during the 60's the Square was cleared and is now a Business Trading Estate.

Of all the many friends and neighbours I knew in those happy days, I know not of their whereabouts, this was one of the most unpleasant aspects of war, we all in our way served in WW2, we drifted apart never to make contact again.

Once more we moved house, the local council rehoused most of the inhabitants, some even moved back to the Square after the prefabs' were built. We were fortunate my father was working part time for my future father-in-law in his business as a Furniture Removal Contractor. Harry Burman was his name, he owned four houses in Clapham and Brixton, and fortunately 139 Bedford Road, Clapham was vacant. 139 was the end but one of a row of early Victorian cottages, the owners wanted to move from London to escape the bombing and Harry had bought the house from them. This was the first time we had a house to ourselves, the only stipulation of tenancy was that two of the rooms upstairs had furniture stored in them from bombed homes, father was asked to keep an eye on the furniture for such damage as mildew.

On the ground floor there was a sizeable sitting room at the front, there was a back bedroom and a kitchen with a scullery, upstairs there

An Apprenticeship to Life

was three bedrooms and a small box room, one of the rooms and the box room had the stored furniture in them. There was a small front garden and a large rear garden; the lavatory was outside attached to the house with a side extension with a sink in it.

The house was very near Ellerslie Square, and much nearer to the pub', this suited my parents very well. My parents had the back bedroom and I slept in the front room on a put-u-up, this then, was the house I lived in until my call up to the Royal Navy in 1943.

Our occupation of 139 was throughout the rest of the war. We received one blasting from a bomb dropped in Acre Lane, this resulted in damage to the roof at the join between 139 and 141, water ingress occurred which damaged the furniture in store. We also had a new front door and frame, plus all the windows were extensively repaired, my collection of Bing Crosby records was smashed when the piano was turned over onto them.

Ironically, although it is said that alcohol kills, in the case of both bombings that we suffered, it may have saved our lives, we were all at the pub' when the houses were blitzed, my parents inside and I outside.

Due to the two bombings our furniture became less and less until we were left with the bare essentials, later in the war the local W.V.S. (Women's Voluntary Service) gave us some good furniture and crockery, but no Bing Crosby records, I was much peeved about that. Of course I blamed Hitler.

The structural damage became worse. And so the upper rooms became uninhabitable through extreme dampness, the stored furniture was moved away and the upper rooms were shut off.

Taking a glimpse in the future, in 1958 the house was compulsory acquired by Wandsworth Council to enable a roundabout to be constructed at the junction of Kings Avenue, Bedford Road, Acre Lane, and Clapham Park Road. I last saw the house in 1970 and it was still boarded up, a pity, as this house could easily have been repaired to help ease the housing problem in the 50's.

139 was the first house in which I had my own den or shed which I built with the aid of my pals, we were able to find all the timber we needed from bombed sites, we also made a covered walk way to the lavatory, this was a great help in wet weather.

The two gardens were full of lovely rose bushes which were always admired by passers by, they were a cheerful sight in a drab wartime world. Father, taking advice from an ignoramus friend heavily pruned at the wrong time of the year and could not understand why they died, so ended our rose gardens.

I must relate a strange tale whilst I am on the subject of dwellings. About 1958, my wife and I rented a first floor flat at 28 Santley Street, Clapham. Our landlord was my wife's bridesmaid, Mary Creasey; Mary and her husband Bill were firm friends of ours until they both passed away. It was strange that during the initial jottings of this book I had a strange feeling that when I was 8 to 10 years old when we lived in Strathleven Road I had a suppressed memory of an elderly lady coming through the front door dressed in Salvation Army uniform. I was talking to Mary one evening and she mentioned that her grandmother lived at 1 Strathleven Road and had the first floor flat some years ago, and that the landlord's name was Rogers. I replied that she couldn't have lived in that flat because my family did and that Rogers was my Uncle Jim, we compares times and dates and it transpired that when Mary's grandmother moved out we moved in. Further discussion revealed that sometimes when we were living at Camden Town and visiting Uncle Jim, my parents went with Aunt Win round to the pub for a midday drink on Sundays and left me with Uncle Jim. Because the elderly lady upstairs was deaf her visitors used to ring Uncle Jim's bell for him to let them in, they were Mary's two aunts, one was always in Salvation Army uniform, hence the Salvation Army lady entering the home. When we visited Brixton I was often told not to make a noise because the lady up stairs was asleep. She was, from this story, Mary's grandmother Mrs Weatherly. When we took over her flat she moved to Manor Road, Clapham where she died in 1935 aged 75. Stranger than fiction?

STREET VENDORS AND OTHERS

One colourful part of life that is almost extinct was the large and varied number of street traders who called virtually at ones door to sell their goods and services.

During my early years my favourites were perhaps the organ grinder and the barrel organ, these seemed to die out in the mid-thirties.

Late Saturday night street markets in Brixton were full of cheerfulness and bustle, the hiss of the gas pressure lamps and the calls of the vendors with the ever presence of the barrel organ brings upon me a nostalgia that grows each year. Of course the pleasure this gave me was probably not a pleasure to my parents and thousands of others like them who were trying to make ends meet, there were no big wage increases each year as there are today. Father was a lead man with one of the big butchers in the market, the butcher would call out to the crowd, "ere, ow abart this, two legs of lamb and a couple of shoulders—5/-, no? how abart you sir" he would point to my father, " ere, four and a tanner then, no? awl right four bob then" father would nod his head, push forward for his meat and pay his 'four bob', this would 'break the ice' and the butcher would suddenly have all the customers he needed to get rid of his meat. In the days without cold storage perishable foods had to be sold because they would not keep until Monday. Of course the butcher and father would meet later in the local and father would get his 'four bob' back, they had known each for years.

Twice a day the paper man would come round the streets carrying a huge bag from his shoulder, he carried 'The Evening News', 'The Evening Standard', and 'The Star'. If you gave him an order for something different, he would deliver it to your door. I could never understand why the newsvendors were such wizened men, and yet carried such large and heavy bags. He sold his papers not by calling at each door but by waiting at a street corner and calling out his wares, always as one word, thus, "Newstarstandard". Each vendor had clearly defined areas, and never impoached on any other round. Newsvenders received their supplies from the wholesalers who dumped large bundles of newspapers at pre arranged places regardless of the weather, these bundles were often to be seen at street corners, no one ever interfered with them.

Sunday deliveries were done house to house by paperboys, in the course of time I played my part doing a paper round. In the better off roads and streets the Sunday boy delivered the week end papers to each house, it was also the Sunday boy's job to collect the paper money each week.

My pals and I worked for a Mrs Hunter who had a newsagents shop in Clapham Park Road, she was a very canny person and would not have the two same boys work the same round, one boy would deliver the newspapers and the other would collect the money, no two boys were allowed to pair permanently, she had a theory that all boys were fiddler's, cheek, as if we would. I was her favourite, but only because I lived at that time very near the shop and I was always willing to do an extra round if anyone dropped out. I never let a penny pass me by.

I can remember seeing very few match boy's, they were really characters from the Victorian and Edwardian periods, but I well remember seeing match men who travelled the pub's in the evening. They were usually little nondescript men who had a tray hung from their necks. On the tray there were two types of matches, the ordinary brown headed match and the red headed match called 'Swan Vestas', the ordinary were 1d a box and the 'Swans' were 2d a box. Pipe smokers particularly favoured 'Swans', as they burnt a bit longer than the ordinary match. Also on the tray one would see various types of shoe and boot laces, strips of five collar studs and shirt buttons, the studs are now seldom seen having gone completely out of fashion. Often a match man would carry a dozen or so mixed ties and braces around his neck. I felt sorry for these men who were after all trying to scrape a living, as soon as they were spotted by the publican there would be a shout of "Oy" with a raised arm and a finger pointing to the door. They also sought customers from theatre and cinema queues; they were given short shrift and abuse no matter where they sought their customers. Even in the street markets if they stood and sold their wares the patrolling policeman would move them on because they were unlicensed. I felt it was a shame, after all they had to make a living, they served a purpose and many of them were ex-servicemen from the First World War.

A great part of the labour force was casual labour, each morning there were queues outside factories and other places that had fluctuating labour needs, and there were no full employment conditions then. From each queue the manager or foreman would select his required number then the rest were turned away. I can remember this system existing as late as 1952 at a local pie factory, of course there was not the level of National assistance that one can obtain now, yet people found sufficient work to exist although a mere existence it was.

The working class man was a proud person, and was reluctant to take a handout, he took whatever work came along, and was glad of it, and yet he always found time and money to have a pint in the pub.

My father-in-law often used casual labour, he was a Removal Contractor and his labour requirements fluctuated greatly, he had a list of reliable men and sent word round when he needed them, this was quite a common practice to have such an arrangement. Then, as now, the men took a day off from their job as 'sick' to work with pa-in-law, moonlighting is not new.

The man our pets waited for twice weekly was the cats meat man, his cry of "Walla Walla cats meat" meant one would soon see a group of cats of all sizes and colours following the man and his basket on a bicycle. The basket was in a frame at the front of the tradesman's type bicycle. On the top of the basket was a board on which he cut up the horseflesh (which was the cat's meat). Slices of meat were pierced with a wooden skewer and sold for 2d, enough for a couple of days.

The "Any old iron" man usually came round with a costermongers barrow, he was rather particular what he accepted, he always preferred clean cast iron, he was reluctant to take enamelled iron, but loved anything made of lead.

The Rag and Bone man would take anything. He came round with a horse and cart and ringing a large hand bell, and had an abbreviated cry, "Ragabone" he would give a goldfish away in exchange for rags. Many a mother missed a dress in exchange for a goldfish. Sometimes there would be a tiny roundabout on the cart whereby small children could have a ride instead of a goldfish. The rag and bone man would take 12 jam jars for a fish, we discovered that one of the shops in Acre Lane would pay a ½d for a clean jar. Now we started collecting jars from neighbours and relatives by the box full. Then the shopkeeper stopped taking them in, and so we went to another shop, until enough was enough and no one wanted jars anymore. People however kept dumping jars at 'Niggers' back yard gate until his mother told us to get the pile of jars out of her yard, we did a deal with the rag and bone man, he gave us Half a Crown (2/6d) for over 200 jars! Needless to say it was a long time before we dabbled in jam jars again.

Sunday afternoons, just after lunch, we saw the winkle man come round with a tray on his head. The tray always had 'J.Lyons & Co Ltd' on the side of it. Some years later, when I worked for J. Lyons, I often wondered how many trays Lyons lost in a year. The trays were about 24" wide and 60" long and quite heavy. The winkle man had all kinds of shellfish in the tray, winkles, cockles, shrimps, whelks and mussels; they were all sold by the half or full pint. The vendor had a peculiar cry, I can only describe it as "Icty Bicty Bor", he was a foreign man and spoke a funny language, Uncle Jim said he was a Croat, but he understood English well. Father always had a ½ pint of winkles, I hated them and still do, and yet I love cockles. All on the tray were 4d a pint, the same price as a pint of beer.

Although the large dairy combines had most of London's families as customers, there were still the small dairymen selling their wares around the streets. He had a pram type of barrow, and on board there was a large churn with a brass tap, there was always a long handled gill measure. Butter and eggs were carried in small quantities as well as cream. The dress of the milkman was boots with full leather gaiters, a straw boater and a blue and white apron; his cry was always "Milko".

The United Dairy (pre Unigate) milkman had a horse and milk float, I often helped out on Sundays collecting empties from the door steps and carrying them to the float, another 1/- for three hours work.

The bakers deliveryman pulled a heavy two-wheeled barrow, this was of the covered in type with two doors at the back delivered bread, rolls and cakes.

There were trays fitted in the top half for cakes and rolls, the lower half was full of bread. These barrows are now collector's items. The local

Typical milk barrow

An Apprenticeship to Life

man was employed by Bamfords the bakers in Acre lane and when he came down Lyham Road, and because of the barrows weight, it began to run freely. The barrow man then took up a peculiar stance between the shafts which became a long loping stride which took him a long time to bring the barrow to a halt. Once he was under way we lads ran behind, opened a door and helped ourselves to a bread roll, all he could was to trot on and swear at us. Eventually a lock was fitted to the doors and our free eats came to an end.

The baker's man had a nick name, 'Quilpy', from a description of a character of Dickens. I discovered years afterwards that 'Quilpy' was my wife's uncle by marriage.

He never ever connected me to the boys who used to 'nick' his rolls.

Another tradesman who is now long defunct was the Glassman; he carried a large wooden frame on his back, and had a large bag of tools. His cry was "Winders", note "Winders" and not "Windows", on the frame he carries all sizes of glass panes, and when he was repairing a ground floor window he always had an audience of children trying to scrounge a piece of putty.

Sometimes he came round with the Chair mender, he repaired woven seats and backs of chairs. He took a chair into the street and sat on the kerb to mend it. He carried a tool bag with the bundles of raffia hung around his neck.

The scissors and knife grinder man had a very ingenious barrow, it was on two wheels with two shafts and had a deep box fitted. The box had an open top with a large grinding wheel evident. When there was work for him to do he placed a board across the top of his box, climbed aboard and sat behind the grinding wheel. There was a treadle in the box and a driving belt, once he started grinding he set up a merry shower of sparks. As we watched the sparks twinkled all over us, no one ever told us to stand clear because any of the sparks could have done untold damage to our eyes.

Our coalman was an obliging person, often tradesmen were surly people, not so our coalman. He had a less taxing job than the coalman had when we lived at Camden Town, as we were now on the first floor and not on the third floor. Our coal bin was now out in the back garden next to Uncle Jim's, they both held 5 cwt', I remember that coal was 11½d a Cwt', the same price as a gallon of ROP petrol. Here I must explain that ROP was Russian Oil Products, the cheapest available. Best house coals was 1/1d a Cwt'. Many of the coalmen were not young men, and yet they did such a hard dirty job. Of course they expected a tip if they had to carry it up stairs, if there was no tip, then the next time the coal would be upended onto the path for the householder to take it in himself. At least the job was regular and many men and their horse remained together for years. The coal cart was really a heavy wagon, and the wagons that took the coal to the depots were pulled by two heavy horses, however many depots were based in the railway sidings, where many men were kept busy just sacking up coals for the next day's deliveries. At the sidings there were small solidly built brick offices for the various coal merchants, usually they had a large board placed on the roof from end to end with the coal merchants name on it. The name that I remember most is 'Hutchinson'. Later in the 30's the 'GasLight & Coke Company' had the monopoly with coal and coke sales in London.

When the coalman delivered the coal it was always paid for in cash, he had a large satchel hung from his shoulder which contained the money and his book, his dress was traditional dating back to the Victorian era. He wore heavy boots, thick corduroy trousers with a belt tightly buckled below each knee, a thick flannel shirt without a collar, over the shirt was usually a tatty waistcoat. Most traditional of all was his hat, this was made of leather, it likened to a bowler hat without a brim, but attached to the back of the hat was a long leather flap as wide as his shoulders, this reached down to his waist. This protected his back from the lumps of coal protruding through the sacks. Overall the coalman had a smell of a mixture of coal, leather, and tar, to a young lad a comforting and warm smell that was like sitting around the coal fire on a winters night. The sack was made of strong woven hemp, it was then treated with a mixture of carbon black and vegetable oil, carbon black is a powder of great penetrating powers it was mixed with the oil and took a long time to dry, but the sack became waterproof and tough. Each sack was examined and had a metal seal fastened to it to prove that it contained a ½ or a whole Cwt' of coal. Each wagon had a pair of scales at the rear to weigh the sacks if necessary; I never saw the scales in use.

Coal Company horses were well looked after and well fed. One of my great delights was to see the horses about midday with their fodder bags hanging on their heads with their noses inside, when they had nearly finished they would toss their head high to get at the last morsel.

Another dirty job was that of the dustman, before the days of protective clothing he dressed similarly to the coalman, but without the head protection. In South London there was a unique system of interchanging the dust carts. The carts were about 8ft high, open topped, with a pair of doors full width across the back, short ladders were hooked to the tops of the sides to enable the dustmen to climb the ladders and tip the dust bins over the top into the cart, which were 18ft long. The cart was mounted on very small solid rubber wheels and was horse drawn. Two chains replaced the shafts that a normal cart would have, and the chains were part of the horse's harness. When the cart was full the dustmen were met at pre-arranged places by a strange looking lorry; it was made by Pagefield, a now defunct marque. It had a half cab, just sufficient for a driver, at the back there was a frame mounted on the chassis, this was able to lift up from the front by means of a hydraulic ram. On the frame were two channels or 'U' shaped rails, these had extensions that were pulled out manually, and when the ram was extended it had the effect of creating a ramp that the dustcart was pulled up on by means of a winch. Once the cart's wheels were secure within the channels the ram was lowered, the extensions pushed in and locked, and the whole took on the appearance of an ordinary box lorry. Before the forgoing was activated the lorry had already lowered an empty cart to the roadway to enable the dustmen to carry on with their job. Of course a captive onlooker was always the horse.

The whole changeover operation took just 10 minutes, I was fortunate that this took place alongside our back garden wall in Ellerslie Square, the operation always looked precarious, and I always waited for the cart to fall off the rails, not once did this happen. The contractors name was 'Surridge', at the time of writing they were still in existence, removing rubbish, it was an operation far ahead of it's time and yet so simple.

The Sweep had a dirty job; it was also a dirty job inside the house. He came round at regular intervals on a box tricycle, he dressed almost the same as the dustman, his method was to fix a sheet across the fireplace, and the sheet had a hole in it where he pushed his brush rods through. The job was done when the brush appeared out of the top of the chimney. Because of the daily use of the fire for cooking even in the summer time, there were masses of accumulated soot; the brush brought this down usually with bits of brick and mortar, the canes were removed, the hearth roughly swept up, and that was the job done. The sweep took the soot away, unless there was a request to keep it as there was a ready market for soot to allotment holders, which increased his fee of 2/-. After he had departed the housewife was faced with almost a spring clean. The sweep cleaning the chimney was the easy part; the hard part was mother having to clean not only the room but also the landing and the top few stairs. Soot penetrated everywhere; there would be a layer of black dust all over the room.

It was dangerous to leave a chimney more than a year before it was swept as they easily caught alight, it seemed odd that a product of combustion would burn, but burn it will, with such force. It was almost a weekly occurrence that one would see a chimney burning, sometimes the Fire Brigade would be called much to our delight. If you decided to deal with the fire yourself there was a set procedure. The fire should be doused with water and put out, it helped if a packet of salt could be thrown on the fire before anything is started. Then a large cloth of any kind should be soaked in water and held tightly across the opening of the fireplace until the roaring stopped. The cloth could be a tablecloth, a blanket, anything that was large enough. When the fire was extinguished there was usually a terrible mess to clear up.

A burning chimney was a frightening experience, we had one just after we moved to Brixton, when it caught alight it roared and turned into a loud whistle the chimney had not been swept for years.

The most noticeable thing of a burning chimney was it's smell, it's odour, it would carry over a whole district, the street or road in which it occurred would become full of dense smoke. To me, as a young lad I was fascinated with railways, the smoke reminded me of locomotives. If we were playing in the street and the smell of a burning chimney came upon us we would run from street to street looking for it, we would stand gazing until the flames came out of the chimney pot.

There is a tale of a small boy who went to a grocer's shop and asked for a packet of salt, the grocer said, "Do you want table salt or cooking salt"? the boy replied "Don't muck about guv', mum's got the chimney on fire".

CHAPTER 5

BUSSES – TRAMS – TRANSPORT - ROAD REPAIRS

THE WATER CART - THE FOOD WE ATE

BUSSES – TRAMS – TRANSPORT

An occasional treat during the summer months was a trip to Richmond on Thames. This was by bus from Acre lane on route 37, or from Clapham Park Road on route 137. Before busses became operated by the London Passenger Transport Board (L.P.T.B.), there were many private companies plying for passengers on the same routes, there were many fast runs being done against stiff opposition. One such company I remember travelling on was the 'Chocolate Express' so called because of it's chocolate and cream livery. This company had the latest design of buses with pneumatic tyres, they were open topped with a windscreen at the front, if you stood up there would be a lovely breeze. For a short while the 'Chocolate' busses were on the Richmond route.

The alighting point at Richmond was at Wakefield Road, this was a semi-terminus, there was such a coming and going in those days, the journey took about an hour. When we alighted we walked around Richmond Green to the river bank and strolled along the tow path which went underneath Richmond bridge, at this point the underside of the bridge was very low and always had an air of mystery. From the bridge it was a nice walk to a pub called 'The Pigeons'. This fronted onto the Petersham Road and backed onto the river, there was a nice patio to sit out on, and this was one of the few pubs where I didn't mind waiting outside. There was so much to see and do, the river boat traffic was prolific, whenever I waved I always had my wave returned. Across the road there was Richmond Hill rising and was surmounted by the massive building of the 'Star and Garter' home for disabled ex-servicemen.

About twice a year we had a boat trip to either Hampton Court or Kingston, most of the trips were run by a firm named 'Salters'. These halcyon days seemed endless, for a couple of years my brother was with us on these wonderful day outings.

The route 137 was a new one and was started in the autumn of 1936; it was the first route to use diesel busses. There was much opposition especial from those who lived in Kings Avenue, the houses here were very large detached properties occupied by wealthy families, all of whom had at least one servant, and they just did not want busses passing their doors going to Streatham. Nevertheless the route started and proved popular, so all the fuss about desecrating Kings Avenue came to nothing in spite of the houses being virtually the same as when they were built in the early 19th century by Thomas Cubitt.

After we moved from Camden Town and during the period when we used to visit relatives there, we travelled from Brixton on the route 59 bus to White hall where we alighted just south of the Cenotaph to change on to route 24, this route was the last to use the old 'General' busses, and these still had solid tyres. On these trips I always carried a few drawing pins that I scrounged from Uncle Jim. As we queued to mount the bus I would press one of the pins into the rear tyre in the hope that I would see it one day, alas some one was pulling these out as fast as I pushed them in. The 24's had an open rear staircase, I loved to climb the narrow twisting stairs whilst the bus was moving, father and I travelled on top while mother sat inside. It was traditional to call the top deck 'Outside' and the lower deck the 'Inside', this applied to trams as well. We always changed busses at Whitehall, although the 59 bus from Brixton went direct to our destination, it went by a longer route.

It was remarkable to see men remove their hats or touch their forelock as the 24 bus passed the Cenotaph as a sign of respect for the fallen in WW1. Today people seldom turn their heads let alone remove their caps or hats and yet the dead increased another 1,000,000 or thereabouts during WW2.

I well remember at 11am on the 11th day of the 11th month each

An Apprenticeship to Life

year, no matter on what day it befell, the whole nation stood for two minutes in silence to remember the dead, even taxi's and lorries stopped at the kerbside. Today this greatest of all ceremonies has been relegated to the nearest Sunday, the whole population is 'Too busy' to stop to remember, it is so regretful and sad.

The top deck on a tram was a peculiar shape; the same both ends, the seat was partitioned off from the stairway. The partition side seat was suitable for five people; the seat opposite curved around the right hand side, front or rear. At the very front the corner caused a clash of knees when the tram was crowded. Each end of the tram when crowed became full of smoke on the top deck, especially during the winter months when all the windows were closed, many more men smoked pipes than today, a pipe full of shag was something to put up with indeed, but multiplied by say 20 it almost created a fog.

Early morning workers trams were nicknamed 'Cougher's specials'. It was very expensive to spit, as some of the older smokers were prone to do, if prosecuted the fine was 40/-s, not much today but nearly a weeks wages then. With the smoke, the pitching of the tram when in motion, and itching eyes, sometimes one was glad to alight at the destination.

Tram seats were reversible simply by pulling the backrest across the seat, it made a curious noise when this was done as the conductor walked the length of the car, Boom, Boom, Boom, on and on, the sound was quite distinctive, this was done of course at the end of every line. If the tram was running on the overhead system and had reached its terminus, the trolley pole had to be reversed. The driver would pull the pole down by its cord and walk right round the tram to attach the pick up to the wire going in the opposite direction. This often meant that he would walk on the pavement or walk round on the opposite side of the road at a radius of 15'.

The tram was the working man's carriage, for the first time the labouring worker was able to find work well away from his home, the fares were cheap and were not an unbearable drain on his income. They allowed him to reach his place of work quickly and more importantly, after a hard days work, he could be home more quickly, indeed at London's busiest junction, Stockwell clock tower, there was a tram every 90 seconds of the day plus a reliable and frequent all night service.

There were special tickets for workmen, these allowed for cheap travel before 7.30am and after 4pm the tickets for this period cost 4d each. It was a return and could be used for the full length of the route providing the ticket was purchased before 7.30am and the return was started after 4pm, these were commonly called the 'Fourpenny workman', a Londoner would call it a, 'forpney one'. Obviously the demand for these trams was great, and the queues were long but the trams were very frequent and at most interchanges and important sites there were centre islands between the tracks which acted as platforms, this made for orderly queues.

I used the 'forpney one' on route 34 for at least two years during the early part of WW2, travelling from Clapham Common to Beaufort Street Chelsea, at the junction with Kings Road; this was about 4 miles each way. The end of Beaufort Street was the terminus for this route, and from there I would catch a N° 11 bus to Fulham, there was a marked difference between tram and bus. The tram was very seldom late in spite of any over night bombing, the timing was such that as the tram arrived a bus would arrive very soon after but never did, and it was either cancelled or would be running late, in which case usually two arrived together. This was the normal situation across London, the trams were reliable and the buses were not, and are still not to this day of writing.

Conductors had a wonderful device hanging from a strap around his shoulders; it was called a 'Bell Punch' machine. Each ticket was of a different colour, this denoted the value of the ticket, the traveller would tell the conductor his destination, the conductor would take a ticket from his ticket clip rack and put the ticket into the machine at the marked boarding point. Then he pushed a small lever and there would be a satisfying 'ting' and a small hole would appear opposite the boarding point on the ticket. The tiny piece of the ticket punched out was collected in a container. If there was any discrepancy between the tickets used and the conductors' takings then the punched out pieces would be counted and valued.

Later tickets only had the Stage number printed on them, from a collectors point of view they were not so interesting as the earlier ones which had the road and street names shown, at one time I had a good collection of the various routes and their values . Tickets varied from a ½d to 1/6d, the smaller denominations were usually clean as they were the most frequently used, but the higher priced ones remained in his rack and became quite tatty before the last one was sold.

Tickets were stapled together in bundles of 30, the rack was a wooden board with six springs fitted on each side, and the springs resembled the spring on a modern clothes peg. In order to make it easier to pull a ticket from the rack. the conductors would remove the staple from a fresh bundle of tickets, At the end of the day the rack and all unused tickets were placed in a small attache case by the conductor, is was locked and secured ready for the conductor to pay in at the depot.

The acceleration of trams was quick or even quicker than most road vehicles; this made it difficult to overtake a tram. Ordinary road vehicles had to halt by law to allow passengers to board and alight, which meant people were crossing the road from the curb to the tram in the middle of the road and vice versa. When the tram started it usually out paced the other road users and at the next stop they would catch up and the process would start all over again. This process was all the more remarkable in view of the tram's weight of 27 tons.

The working man's family was also served cheaply, during the day there was a 4d all day ticket that could be used for any distance and time, providing it was between 9am and 4pm. At weekends there was the 1/- weekend ticket that enabled people to visit each other cheaply, I used this often.

As other traffic increased, the trams became a burden, they caused congestion at places and the rails were dangerous if a vehicle caught a wheel tyre in a rail, the secret, especially on wet days, was to cross a rail at an acute angle. If it was crossed at a fine angle the tyre would drop into the well of the rail, the only way out was to wrench the steering wheel of the car one way or the other. I remember on such a day, when I had a motorcycle, my narrow front tyre caught in one of the rails that emerged from Clapham Tram Depot. It caused me to skid across the road and pavement into a shop front, there was no damage to the shop or myself, but the front forks were bent. After that incident I held much respect for tramlines.

Fog was a terror in those days and in a real 'pea souper' the tram was the only vehicle that could still run, it could not lose it's way and provided it moved slowly it was safe. Only abandoned traffic could stop it. If you knew the trams route number you could follow it home, although there were many times that when a tram turned into its depot a long line of traffic would follow it in.

On such foggy nights the tramway officials lit giant flares at main road intersections, because of the heat from the flare, it caused the fog to rise and create a partial clearance of fog with some visibility.

Just before the outbreak of WW2, many other fare concessions were introduced. there was a special underground fare of 2d for the journey from the Bank and Waterloo, there was a great outcry when this fare was increased to 2½d in 1938, and a 25% increase was unheard of. After 6pm on tram routes, there was a 6d ticket that enabled one to travel all night anywhere in the area South of the Thames, there was a similar ticket for North of the Thames.

Trams run by the L.P.T.B. had a particularly cheap ticket. This was issued Mondays to Fridays, excepting any public holiday, any tram leaving central London termini between 9.30am to 4pm, and all trams scheduled to arrive at central London between 10.30am to 5pm, had a fare of 2d for any length of journey. Even a 1d ticket covered a greater distance than at any other time of the day; these cheap tickets were designed to fill the trams all day instead of just at rush hour times.

There was a unique stretch of rails in London that I have never discovered on any other tram system; this was on Dog kennel hill, Dulwich. This was a very steep part of the system, in the 1920's, because of a brake failure; a tram ran backwards and crashed into a following tram with loss of life. To ensure that this would never happen again, the authorities converted the track into four lines so that a tram would never be on the same track as the one ascending.

To see the tracks going over the brow of the hill was a sight, there was

Trams passing on the 4 track Dog Kennel Hill - South London

'Easing in the shoe' at Brixton Interchange.

nothing but the skyline on the brow, and to watch a tram emerge at the top and then plunge down was exiting

My parents often used 'The Gresham Arms', a pub on the corner of Gresham Road and Brixton Road. At this point the trams changed the electrical supply system from conduit to overhead. I would stand for hours waiting for the trams to approach the switching point, and as each tram did it would throw out from below the car the collection 'Plough'. The driver would then raise the trolley pole to connect to the overhead line and away the tram would go on its journey to Camberwell Green. On the return journey the procedure was reversed, and as the tram drove away the 'Plough' was slowly drawn into the centre rail below the tram.

The overhead line trams could be heard long before they arrived, the wire above made a lovely swishing sound, and if it was raining at night there would be flashes of blue light emitting from the cable as the trolley wheel rode along it and passed the cable joints. Many people claimed that the flashes guided the German bombers during the Blitz, although Brixton and Camberwell had more than their fair share of bombs, this of course was nonsense.

If, through heavy traffic, a tram had to stop when crossing points in the track, it sometimes occurred that the pick up plough halted at a break in the continuity of the current, this rendered the tram immobile. To overcome this problem a short stout pole together with a strong cable with eyes attached at each end were kept at strategic junctions. By these means a following tram could push the stricken tram or a tram in front could pull it with the cable, it was just a case of moving it a few feet to pick up the current. Very seldom was a tram totally immobilised.

One lasting memory of tracks and trams was when I was about 10 years old, I was taken to Chalk Farm Underground station and there let into the roadway was a short length of twin track. I was told that this was the last piece of horse drawn tram track. However years later, I discovered another stretch of horse tram track in Stockwell Road, South London, this time complete with a set of points. The rails turned off the road through an arch between two shops that belonged to Pride and Clark's, a well-known motor cycle dealer, at the back was the remains of a horse tram depot. The lines were still there c. 1955.

It was a rare treat for me to ride in a taxi; we did this sometimes when Uncle Jim obtained complimentary tickets for a West End show that he was working on. Taxi's had a peculiar fare range, for two thirds of a mile or 7½ minutes it was 9d, for each extra one third of a mile or 3½ minutes it was an extra 3d to pay, for any less distance or time it was 3d. For a bicycle, mailcart or pram the fare was 3d. Why a mailcart should be carried in a taxi escapes me, other packages carried outside cost 3d. For each additional person the charge was 6d.

The road surfaces we endured in the 30's was abysmal, there were still miles of roadway surfaced with bitumen, this left the surface with an almost glass like finish when rain was falling, this coupled with tyres made from hard rubber caused many accidents.

Many roads were still surfaced with wooden blocks; great efforts were made during the inter-war years to remove them. The tramways however hindered the road maintenance, the lines were embedded in granite setts between the two rails and also with two lines of setts outside the rails, and with further setts between the tracks, these setts were the responsibility of the tramway companies. The rest of the roadway was cambered steeply into the gutter.

When the roads were resurfaced the wooden blocks were replaced with concrete.

Our local roads were resurfaced annually with tar and gravel, we children hated this as it made skating virtually impossible, the gravel also spread over the pavements, scattered by passing vehicles. On the afternoon of the resurfacing, as soon as we arrived from school we all turned out with household brooms and swept the pavements right round the Square and up Lyham road as far as the furthest 'gang' member. We could then skate as far as any member of our group, the gravel was notorious for damaged hands knees and elbows; falls during this period were common.

It was fascinating to see this method of resurfacing the roads. A large lorry full of gravel would drive down each side of the road, and at intervals men on the lorry would shovel a heap of gravel on to the pavement at roughly 25' intervals, a small trolley containing bitumen was pulled by a smaller lorry. On the trolley was a man working a pump and another controlling a spray. Bitumen was sprayed over the entire road surface and as they passed the gravel piles men would shovel the gravel on to the road with a flick of the wrist that spread the gravel evenly so that it stuck to the bitumen. The men would work along the street from pile to pile, and finally a man would walk each side of the street with a broom and sweep the remains into the gutter. Sometimes a road roller would run up and down the roadway to ensure the grit was bedded down properly.

If the road surface needed repair, a tar boiler would be set up nearby to melt the large blocks of bitumen. Great clouds of smoke would billow from the stack pipe of the boiler; the boiler fire being fed with bitumen chips caused this. When the bitumen was molten it was poured into the cracks in the road surface before the grit was applied.

If any of us had a cold we were told by our mothers to stand as near to the fire as possible, we were told to breathe the bitumen vapours in deeply. It was supposed to help to eliminate the cold, it never did in my case, but then, I always seemed to sniff in more of the smoke from the chimney than from the bitumen.

There was usually about a dozen men employed in the road gang, mostly casual labour, it gave men work and hope. It is said that post war unemployment was caused by the depression, is it not true, this was

A Lambeth water cart

started by man himself creating machines to do the work of men, thus causing an ever increasing downward spiral of redundancy of manpower.

One of the joys of summer was the water cart. Each street was washed down each day. The cart was horse drawn; it had two wheels and a tank behind the Carter. In the period about 1936/7 the horse drawn tank was replaced by a motor vehicle, which drove slowly down the street, the water was dispensed from perforated tubes, which were mounted at the front and rear of the tanker. The water went across the pavement, and sometimes as far as the doorsteps of the houses.

As soon as the tanker appeared off came our plimsoles and socks and we danced along behind the tanker having a lovely spray over legs and feet. The tankers filling point was at the junction of Kings Avenue and Lyham Road. Sometimes the driver would turn the water on slowly to refill the tank, and then walk down to Clapham Park Road for his tea break in the café there. When he did this invariably the tank overflowed creating a flood down the gutter, there was great fun making paper boats to race them and placing our bets with cigarette cards.

During very hot weather, those who had a soapbox cart would put on a swimming costume and wait for the water tank to come round. We would run round to the rear, hook the steering string on to the spray bar lay on the soapbox and be drawn along amidst a lovely shower of cold water.

We were fortunate that the water tank came our way after school hours. The driver was a jolly man who didn't mind how many children were behind his tank, he would never allow anyone in the front of his tank, and he would become very cross if any one defied him.

Water tankers vanished just before the war, I have never discovered why, was it just to economise or was it due to better road surfaces becoming less dusty?

THE FOOD WE ATE

The sweets we were able to buy in the 30's are probably the cause of many bad teeth that the elderly have today, there was little awareness of teeth hygiene then. The range of confectionery was enormous and sweetshops were prolific, almost on every street corner.

A common sweet was the 'Gobstopper', there were three sizes, ¼d, ½d, and 1d, the 1d gobstopper was gigantic, it almost filled one cheek, it was made of hard sugar in multi layers of different colours. They were extremely hard and as one sucked it, it changed colour with the consequence that fingers became sticky, through often taking it out of the mouth to see what colour it was.

Sherbet is a word not often seen today, but can still be found if one searches, my favourite was the sherbet fountain, this was a cardboard cylinder covered with a bright yellow label and filled with the sherbet powder. Protruding from the centre of the cylinder was a liquorice tube, as the powder was sucked into the mouth it created a delightful fizzy sensation, when the powder was consumed the liquorice tube could be eaten. Many times the powder went straight down the throat, and then one could pleasantly choke for a while.

A similar sweet was the sherbet dab, this was a paper cone filled with the powder, in the centre was a stick with a blob of toffee on the end. The toffee was sucked and then dipped into the powder, such delights, all for a ½d.

Broken toffee is hard to find now, in the 30's it could be found everywhere in all shapes and sizes, my buy was ½d worth of mixed broken toffee, usually from the left over pieces of large slabs. A 4lb slab was huge; it was supplied with its own hammer. These had a hammerhead on one side and a cutting head on the other; they were made of cast iron with the maker's name along the handle, usually 'Sharps', as this was the most common toffee to be had. Toffee was seldom broken on a hard surface; large pieces were held by the shopkeeper in the cupped palm of a hand and hit with the hammer. I still have one of the hammers today, a cherished possession from my childhood. Toffee was also supplied as 'splits', this was a sandwich of a flavoured toffee between a top and bottom of ordinary toffee, and the flavours came as, banana, strawberry, vanilla, lemon and raspberry. There was also toffee with nuts and toffee coated with chocolate.

My local shop was really a house just across the road from our house, it was run by a dear kind old lady, her name was Mrs Irons, her husband was a large gruff and grumpy man. Mrs Iron's front room had been converted into a shop with a counter extending toward the front window. She catered for the ¼d and ½d trade for the children, our area was not of the kind where people would buy boxes of chocolates, they would be bought in the larger shops in Acre Lane. On the counter she had six large enamel trays, it was a treat if you were in the shop when the sweet salesman called, he brought in big bags of broken toffee, boiled sweets, and in the winter months a bag of winter mixture. He opened the bags and poured the contents onto the trays, if any dropped onto the floor Mrs Irons would invite any of the children who happened to be there to pick up the pieces, and so have a free helping.

The Irons had a very large Old English Sheep dog, this dog was very docile and had a poor ear for music, and the dog sat by the porch most of the day and never went in until after dark on most nights. Just to annoy Mr Irons we would creep up to the dog after dark, lift one ear and gently blow the highest note from a mouth organ, we then ran like blazes. The dog waited for a few moments and then set up a fearful howling. Of course the howling disturbed the neighbour hood until his owner dragged the dog indoors, even then the racket could be heard. We found out years later that the dog was tone deaf, it could hear the high note but not his master's voice. He cursed the dog as much as he did us boys.

Cigarette sweets were popular, the better quality ones were almost full size and came in packets of 10 or 20, they also had cigarette cards inside. Surprisingly the cards were of good quality, although I never knew anyone to have collected a full set, I suspected that one card was never printed. Along with sweet cigarettes were chocolate cigars, these were not so realistic. There were also liquorice pipes; these had hundreds and thousands on top of the bowl to imitate a real glow. At Christmas time there were 'Smokers Sets' available, all in confectionery. I often wonder how many youngsters were encouraged to smoke the real thing by these imitations?

Another liking I had was for a chocolate bar called 'Double Six', this was a larger than normal bar which had twelve different centres, the wrapper was printed to resemble a domino, hence the name, the bar was priced at 4d, unfortunately the bar did not survive the war.

Toffee apples disappeared after the war, but in the late 80's they re-emerged and are now often seen. In my childhood the toffee apples were made mostly by the sweet shop owner, the apples were large and sweet, today they are small and wrapped in plastic bags, when they are unwrapped a lot of the toffee pulls off with the wrapper. The toffee apple of the 30's was dipped in toffee and then stood on a tray that had been greased, usually about a dozen to a tray, when they had cooled there was a lovely ridge of hard toffee that one could nibble before savouring the apple. It was delightful paying the ½d, and then taking your time to choose the best one, a simple thing, but so nice.

Ice cream was mostly sold from barrows or tricycles on street rounds. The vendors were from Wall's, Eldorado, and best of all to my taste Marcantonio's, this was a local ice cream but prevalent to South London, the ice cream they sold was a soft creamy texture always sold in a cornet, or for a 1d you could have a double cornet.

Wall's made a harder ice cream, this was sold mainly as small 'bricks' for a penny, and for your penny you were given two wafers the same size as the brick. there were other sizes, for example for 6d there was a large brick which would slice into four nice portions, the drawback with this was that it had to be eaten immediately, simply because in the 30's only wealthy families had refrigerators. Wall's also sold a product called 'Snofrute' and 'Snocream', this was very popular, it was of the frozen water type of ice cream, it was sold in a triangular carton from which you could push the ice up from one end.

Wall's ice cream was sold from tricycles painted in a blue and white livery; the box on the tricycle was insulated and kept cold with cardice blocks. The salesman rode from street to street ringing a loud bell, and on the front of the box was a sign which read 'Stop me and Buy One'. This was the Wall's slogan for many years.

I did not like Eldorado's, it had a different flavour to the others, Marcantonio's was by far, my favourite, with a flavour likened to the modern 'Mr Whippy'.

Whilst on the subject of ice, before the domestic 'fridge' was available to ordinary homes and shops there was a need for bulk supply of ice, especially to fishmongers. Ice was delivered to the shops by an open lorry carrying large blocks covered with canvas sacks to help to slow down the melting process. According to the shops needs the driver would split the blocks with a large icepick. If we were near we would gather around the lorry waiting for pieces to fly off, and while he was delivering we would scoop up lumps of ice that was laying on the back of the lorry. The driver carried the ice block by a large pair of tongs. The company was Carlo Gatti Ltd; they carried ice all over London and have long gone out of business.

Nothing was wasted in my young days. For a ½d one could buy a big bag of sweet crumbs, the secret of this was to sit on the kerb and hit the bag with a piece of wood, this compacted the sticky crumbs, then pieces would be broken off and chewed. Biscuit crumbs could be bought for a ½d, but broken biscuits were dearer, and in the fried fish shop a ½d bag of cracklings could be had, on a cold winter night we thought a bag of hot cracklings was luscious.

In some sweet shops there was a lemonade machine installed. On the counter there was a large glass dome filled with water, under the counter there was a gas cylinder, I recall it was filled with Carbon Di-oxide (Co_2). The nice taste of this drink was it's vanilla flavour, the powder was put into the glass which was then filled with the fizzy water as bubbles passed up through the dome. I have not seen any of these machines since the war, many of course must have been destroyed and were not replaced.

Still on the subject of drinks. During the fairs held on Hampstead Heath at Bank holidays and Christmas time, a glass of hot Sarsaparilla could be had for a 1d. I have not tasted this drink since 1937. I have been told that it is on sale at County Fairs although I have never seen it, however the travelling fair is slowly disappearing and so I suppose will Sarsaparilla.

As a child I enjoyed the walk from the horrible house we lived in to Ken Wood and Hampstead Heath, and on to the heath fairs, during one of these walks I remember seeing a placard outside a newsagent's reporting 'Quetta Earthquake'. I was full of curiosity and asked my father where Quetta was, he did not know and was not interested. The next time I saw Uncle Jim he told me. And gave me a geography lesson, many people died in that catastrophe, and the year was 1934. So, on with 'What We Ate'.

Queens Crescent had a large street market on Saturdays. Always packed with people, late at night auctions were held at the butchers and fish mongers stalls, usually started after the pubs closed, many of the stalls were open until midnight. Because most meat and fish vendors only had unrefrigerated cold rooms, it was best to sell off as much as possible. The butcher would hold up a joint of meat and call out "ere we are, five bob", if there were no takers "Nar then 'ow abart four and a tanner", he would gradually reduce the price until it sold. Often he would throw in a pound of sausages, or a couple of chops. Father often came home with half a leg of lamb for less than 1/-.

The bakers on the corner of Queens Crescent and Ashdown Street (Hemmings) were good to me when mother sent me to them on Monday mornings for the weeks bread, I would go down with a sixpenny piece, and in return I would be given three quarten loaves of bread, which, to carry, I had to hold my arms out straight. A quarten loaf was about twice as long as today's standard loaf, then on top of the bread I was given a big bag of stale cakes. One must remember that the bread was baked only the Saturday afternoon before I bought it on the Monday morning before I went to school. The cakes were very eatable, usually ten to twelve and were of various kinds such as rock cakes. coconut cakes, small Madeira cakes, bath buns and current buns and so on.

When I left the bakers I used to pause at the side wall and gaze up at a memorial on which was a list of names of those who were killed and wounded in WW1. My father's name was on the top of the wounded list, I was always so proud of that. I last saw the memorial about 30 years ago and often wonder where it is today, but once more I digress.

Vegetables were a great part of our diet, often without meat. The favourite was two pennyworths of 'potherbs'. These were mixed vegetables, for the 2d there was a few potatoes, a Swede, a turnip, a few carrots, and a couple of onions. If we were lucky there would be six pennyworth of stewing stake from the Saturday market. Add this all together and the result was a good Hot Pot for two days.

Fish was another food that would not keep over a weekend; this as meat was sold off cheap on a Saturday night. My joy was soft roe on toast, a large handful and more was bought for 2d. Half a dozen big bloaters for 3d, best kippers at 2d a pair, I wondered why they were always sold in pairs?

Paraffin pressure lamps lighted stalls, these burned with a very bright light and with a roaring hiss, which was to me a satisfying sound.

Bread was never toasted until it became hard, it was then spread with margarine, never with butter, that was only for the better off's. We used 'Crelos'; David Greigs sold this. 'Crelos was the first of the margarines. David Greigs first shop was in Railton Road in Brixton, they expanded to become one of the largest provision store chains in the London area. Then, there was prosperity in Brixton, not racial riots; I cannot remember any of my parent's friends ever being out of work.

Shops always did a good trade and seldom closed through the lack of it, if they did it was usually the fault of the shopkeeper as there were ample shoppers. A trend of those times was to run up a bill and pay up at the end of the week, casually known as 'Putting it on the slate'. Some shopkeepers went out of business simply because they trusted their customers too much who owed him so much that he could not pay his bills, and bankruptcy followed. However, most shopkeepers became of the middle class and had a comfortable living.

Pub's were always full and did a roaring trade, people seldom received a pay rise, but then there was very little inflation, work hours were long, 54 hours was the basic week. There was little sympathy for those who fell ill, and were unable to work. The hardest hit were the women who had lost their husbands and depended on National Assistance and were means tested. Many of them were told to sell their unnecessary effects, such as a piano before any help was forthcoming, many pianos were prudently 'loaned' to a neighbour before the means test inspector visited the home. Pianos were usually family items having been handed down through the years. There were irregular visits from the inspectors to ensure that there was no other income going into the home, such as any earnings, however small, and personal savings were not allowed.

The free food markets that we enjoyed up to 1939 became a very different situation once war broke out.

Food rationing books were issued on the 28th of November 1939, but full rationing did not start until 1942. People were compelled to register with a retailer before 23rd of November 1939. There was a government announcement on the 28th of November 1939 that rationing would start on the 8th of January 1940, although this date became delayed.

The initial ration was 4ozs of bacon or ham, 4ozs of butter each week, and 12ozs of sugar each week, by the end of January the bacon ration was doubled. This in fact became a larger bacon entitlement than most people ate before the war, probably because most people could not afford to buy more. On the 11th of March meat became rationed to 1/10d worth per week to each person over the age of 6 years, the under 6's received a ration of 11d per week.

The larger families with an accumulation of rations were able to buy a joint of meat whereas a single person was restricted to one meat chop and perhaps two sausages. In October 1940 the meat ration went up to 2/2d per week, which we all thought was wonderful, this lasted only a few months however, and then in January 1941 it was reduced to 1/2d per week, it remained at this level for the rest of the war.

In May 1941, jams, syrups, treacles and margarines were fixed at 8ozs per month , in july1941 these were all raised to 1lb. In may1941 cheese was rationed to 1oz per week, although some workers were given 8oz, road workers were included in this extra ration, this caused some disgruntlement because some workers on heavy work were not included and others on lighter work were.

In June 1941 eggs became controlled but not rationed, this meant that there was no entitlement to any eggs, even though the retailer had received an allowance for his customers and area. This of course meant that eggs were kept 'under the counter' and were never put on display. After the shopkeeper or owner had earmarked eggs for his own family he would allow his best customers a few eggs, there were of course shopkeepers who were fair and offered his customers one egg per person until they were gone. How did I know about 'eggs for the family'? My wife's uncle was a grocer.

There were never sufficient eggs for everyone to be satisfied. I remember my maiden aunt being given two eggs which she promptly dropped when unloading her shopping, they dropped onto the floor and smashed, the precious eggs were scrapped up from the linoleum, nothing in those days was wasted.

It became customary for people to take part of their ration with them when they visited friends or relatives, up to recent years this habit still continued but is now dying as memories of the 40's fade away.

A national loaf was introduced and immediately the taste of bread changed, I hated the taste, it was full of chaff and so unlike the bread I knew as a child, even though our bread was the so called stale loaf as I described earlier.

Many people started keeping their own hens, my father did. My wife's father also had half a dozen hens, proper chicken food was unobtainable so the birds were fed on scraps of waste food, none of the hens were the plump ones of pre and post war years, they were scrawny and laid small eggs with very pale yellow yolks. Certainly they were not worth killing for the table, there was just no meat on them. Neighbours sometimes gave their scraps in exchange for an egg or two. Officially, if the egg production exceeded a certain amount the eggs had to be sold to the Ministry of Food. By the end of the war my father-in-law had a small holding with about 250 hens and 50 geese.

Fruit virtually disappeared from shop windows, I recall being given an orange at Christmas time 1941 by Tunesi the greengrocer, I ate it on Christmas day, I still think it was the best orange I have ever tasted. Bananas became unobtainable, everywhere, very young children had never seen one and had to be taught how to eat them after the war. Outside the period of this book, I was being transported to Australia in 1944. When we arrived at Panama onboard the 'Empress of Scotland', a troopship, we were allowed onto the quayside for a while, we found a shed full of hands of bananas hanging to ripen. About 200 RN ratings raided the store and came out with bunches of the fruit, we were all rounded up and ordered back on board ship, and we had bananas tucked in our uniform everywhere. By the time we reached Sydney, the bananas had ripened and had been eaten. The first we had tasted for two years!

Fish and vegetables were left untouched but controlled, and as usual they disappeared 'under the counter', either to reappear to favoured customers or on the 'black market'. This applied especially to seafood, cockles and winkles sold by the street vendor vanished, never to be seen again on the streets. The fried fish and chip shops were severely rationed, most of them closing two days a week, and when they did open they fried until they ran out of fish and then closed for the rest of the night.

Various substitutes appeared such as egg substitute, this was a very bright yellow powder, and when cakes were made of this, they too were bright yellow.

People dug up their back gardens to grow vegetables. At Bedford Road, Clapham we had potatoes, cabbages, tomatoes and other vegetables. Those who had allotments exploited every piece of ground. There even arose reports in local newspapers of thefts of produce from allotments, and allotment growers set up their own vigilante groups to guard the allotments. There sprung up an efficient barter system whereby people exchanged, for example, eggs for cigarettes, and apples for match's etc, yes-even matches were controlled and scarce.

I saved my used cigarette packets as these had all but disappeared; shopkeepers had their supplies delivered loose in boxes of 1000. If one was lucky enough to find a shop that had 'cigs' for sale, the shopkeeper would ask if you had an empty packet, if the answer was no, you would receive them in a paper bag.

Pipe tobacco was very scarce, and usually sold only to long standing customers, of course when shops were blasted during the Blitz, and failed to reopen, then one had a long hunt to find ones favourite brand.

The Government announced that the basic diet to maintain good health was, 12ozs of bread, 16ozs of potatoes, 2ozs of oatmeal, 1oz of fat, and 6ozs of vegetables and two thirds of a pint of milk. Ironically, although people complained of the shortage of food, the nation as a whole, became healthier because of the restricted but balanced diet.

CHAPTER 6

HOBBIES – SCHOOL - PRANKS AND GAMES

RELIGIOUS THOUGHTS - OUR GANG - OUR GIRLS

HOBBIES

Over the decades cigarette card collecting became an institution of the younger years, there is still a large following of those who are now adults.

My first memory of a complete set was of the 1934 John Players 'Cricketers' series.

Being only nine years of age, with heroes like Larwood, Verity, Oldsmith, Bradman, Sutcliffe and Hobbs, I was in my glory each time I acquired a new card. Most cards were collected simply by accosting men in the street and saying, "Got any fag cards please mister?"

The slightly built boys were invariably more successful than the bigger lads. I was more successful than my pals were because I was a bit of a runt with a mischievous look; at least I like to think that is the reason for my success. I suppose it was really that people took pity on me. If I gained less than 25 a day it was usually because it was raining, I suppose it really was a seasonal hobby.

I had a regular patch, or really two regular patches as I shared one with my school pal Billy, this was a useful arrangement because if another lad tried to crash in on our patches the two of us could bully him away. Billy and I always equally shared our gains. Our patches were the two bus stops in Acre lane, opposite each other, here we had Nos 35, 35a, 37, 42, 45, and 45a bus routes, all of which were very busy between

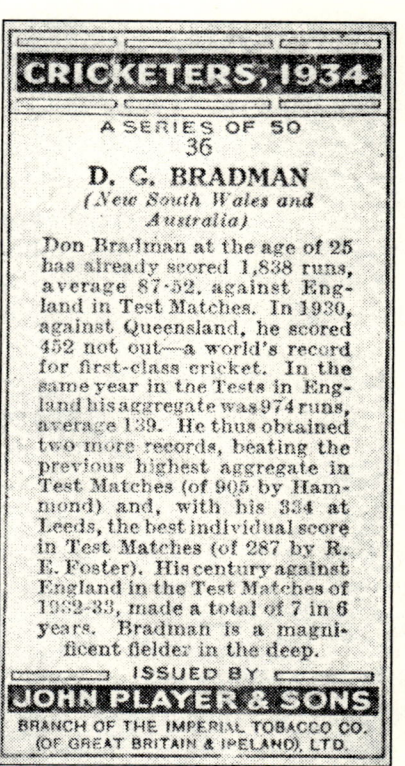

'Got a fag card please mister?'

5.30pm and 6.30pm . Many men knew me by sight and always travelled on the lower deck or 'inside' as it was called, this was useful because as soon as they alighted they would take out their cigarettes and then I would pounce on them. I often wondered why they didn't save their cards for their own children, I couldn't believe that all of them didn't have any. There were many doubles collected, these were exchanged with other collectors on a basis of one for one or even one for more than one, depending on the scarcity of the one that was needed.

There was much knowledge to be gained from cigarette cards; there were series on sports, gardening, army , navy, trains, and a hundred and one other things, even when the war broke out on air raid precautions.

The tobacco companies issued albums to hold each set; each was usually of 50 cards. We did not like the albums and considered a set stuck in an album to be inferior to a loose set. The cards were of a very high quality; it could not be said that any one card was better than another. Early cards were not gummed on the reverse side, these lasted up to about 1937, after that the gummed ones became more prevalent. The later ones had to be stored absolutely dry, there was no greater disaster than a set of good cards stuck together.

My Uncle Jim always purchased his cigarettes in boxes of 25 or 50, I did see him once with a drum of 100, he smoked only W.D.& H.O.Will's 'Goldflake'. There were always extra cards appropriate to the number of cigarettes bought. Gallaghers issued some doublesized cards but only in the 20's packets, some sets were hand coloured.

I still have in my collection some issues printed on silk, these were issued by Hill's circa 1933/34 and depicted flags of the world and prominent people. These are in mint condition, far better than the remnants of the ordinary cards of my collection of long bygone days.

It is pleasing though that in recent year's tea companies started issuing cards in packet of tea. Early ones issued by Lyons depicting aircraft were of excellent quality, but the ones issued by Brook Bond often had off centre print errors and machine marks, Alas even they have now gone.

The boy of today has never known the excitement of the hunt for an elusive card; they can be bought from dealers and auctions. What boy needs cards when he can have a £600 computer, it may transpire that today's dads are the boys and the boys are the grown up's of today.

Bus tickets were another collector's item of yesteryear that cost nothing to obtain. We tried the impossible task of collecting a complete series. One easy way of obtaining some of the millions of different tickets was to wait until the bus stopped and discharged it's passengers, then as it moved off, jump on the platform and kick the bottom of the used ticket box. This caused the door on the bottom to open and discharge its contents, a flood of nice tickets that blew out as the bus gathered speed.

We then had the task of dodging traffic in order to collect the tickets, we only had need to do this once a day as we had then enough tickets to sort.

I spent many hours matching serial numbers, hours that should have been spent on homework for school. Wasted hours that even now in retirement I regret, yet somehow I feel that childhood should be spent

An Apprenticeship to Life

on pursuits that grownup's are not interested in, because pursuits that a grownup considers useless can be of great interest to a boy.

One of the joys of my young life was my stamp collection. I started collecting them when I was 9 years old, I started them as most small boys did with 1d and 2d packets. I used to gaze in awe at stamps marked at 1d and 2d each and thought how expensive they were. The world of 1d blacks and 2d blues was far away from me in those days, those days of forever finding information about new stamps that I had bought.

My first purchases were bought from 'Hunters' newsagents, where later I did my first paper boys round up to the outbreak of war. Her packets of stamps ranged from 1d up to 5/-, the 5/- packet contained over 1000 stamps. I remember the packets contained an extraordinary number of Chinese stamps which gave me the impression that the inhabitants of China wrote more letters than any other country in the world, I imagined that hordes of Chinamen were sitting writing all day. No doubt the prolific number of stamps was and still is due to the vast number of people living in China.

These packets were not as interesting as the one's I purchased a little later in life from an old gentleman who had a second hand bookshop on the hill in Clapham Park Road. I was never sure if the old chap owned the shop or just rented a part of it to sell his stamps, on occasions there was a younger man in the shop who seemed to know more about books than stamps.

The shop was dark and dingy, as indeed the old man appeared at times. He had boxes of packets from a 1d upwards, but behind the partition curtain there were shelves containing books of stamps which were not for small boys. He invited people more of his own age into the back room, I often saw them earnestly discussing stamps. I often wondered how long they stayed there, I discovered much later that the room was a meeting place for a stamp club.

I spent hours there sorting through his boxes of ten for a penny, of course I was not alone, there was invariably three or four boys sorting through the boxes. The old chap gave us valuable advice, one advice I well remember was 'Collect what you are interested in, not what you should collect'. One thing that was a help was that every time a penny was spent he gave one a ticket and when 12 tickets were taken back they were exchanged for a small packet of stamps. He was such a kindly man, any strange stamp that was taken to him was quickly identified and a short lesson was delivered on its origin and value.

I gradually built up a large collection of the whole world; it was not a valuable collection but an interesting one. I dreamed over my stamps and read and re-read any second hand stamp magazines that I obtained, mostly I dreamed of the countries from which the stamps came from, especially the stamps of the 'Federated Malay States' these depicted a tiger leaping in the jungle. I imagined that the whole of the peninsula was jungle, I realised during the war that only parts were so.

By the time I was called up in 1943 my collection numbered many thousands and had survived the two bombings. My collection along with all of my books disappeared while I was overseas in the Pacific area in 1945. My parents could not or would not account for my loss, I believe they were sold to fulfil their insatiable appetite for drink, and so I was informed later of their belief that I would not return from the war, but that is another story.

I renewed my interest in the 60's with a much-reduced coverage; I now have a much more valuable collection than that of my youth. I often wish for some of the stamps of my younger days, as they would now be quite rare. I still have them in a way as they are now in my collection of memories.

Friends in Australia and Germany kindle my interest world-wide, stamp collecting breaks all barriers, especially religious and political. It is a very good way of standing back from the 'Daily grind', and above all, I, as most collectors do, dream of obtaining the stamp that is unobtainable.

SCHOOLS

In 1930 I started school in Camden Town, at the old Board school in Carlton Road, I was there for just a few months, and then we moved to Brixton in South London. I then attended Sudbourne Rd Junior School, which was about 15 minutes walk from our home in Strathleven Road.

I had four happy years at Sudbourn Road; I showed no promise while there and of course my happiness was marred by the death of my brother which has been described earlier.

When I was eleven I moved on to the senior school in Lyham road, this was Parkside School, please do not be fooled by the term Parkside, it was a simple L.L.C. (London County Council) secondary school.

An Apprenticeship to Life

I did not shine at all in sports, except for one glorious occasion when playing a game of scratch in the school playground, I whacked the ball so hard that it cleared the safety net surrounding the playground and landed high up on the roof of Carter Patterson's depot. The sports master witnessed this and immediately put me into the first eleven. My first and only glory on the field of sport was played at Brockwell Park, here we played Lollard Street from Kennington, I was second bat, and the first bat made one run so I was in. I was clean bowled, out for a duck. The next three matches only added single figures for each innings, and then I was dropped. I was not really sorry; I never excelled in any sport except skating, in which I was one of the best.

My best subject was geography, followed by history. I was poor at maths and English, on the practical side I was good at bookbinding and carpentry. Maths always gave me problems until I became proficient in later years. Oh how I eternally regret my lost years at grammar school, but then I suppose if I had received a good education I would never have been blessed with the drive to get on with life against any odds that came my way.

My form master was a tyrant with bad teaching methods that my form friends and myself could learn nothing from. We were all in fear of him. When he was on play ground duty there was dullness in our play in case for some reason we upset him. He was in his 60's when I joined his form and I quickly found out that he punished for the sake of punishment and was prone to commit sadistic acts. His favourite way of venting his fury was to swing a police type whistle which was on the end of a leather thong, and crash it on the poor pupils head. Needless to say I only suffered this once, I made sure I didn't offend him again. He treated a new boy to the usual swing and a bang on the head, so he thought, but the boy moved his head and the whistle hit the lads ear and nearly severed the lobe. With blood everywhere and with a huge uproar going on, the poor lad was sent to hospital, the teacher disappeared and we were sent home for the afternoon. My mother was convinced that it was I that had done something wrong. Why me?

The next morning we had a temporary teacher and indeed he was our form master for the next few weeks, in time we gained a new form master who was vastly different from the demon we had before.

Under our new master we all improved our learning, mainly because of his patience and understanding, I never knew him to loose his temper, certainly I improved so much, that at 13½ years old I sat and gained a free scholarship to grammar school, which I was unable to take up, owing to the interference of Adolf Hitler. More of that anon.

My bookbinding prowess came from my father's tuition. He was at one time working for a bookbinding company, his job then was as a sewer in the binding process, he had gained a good knowledge of the other processes which in time he passed on to me. I have now passed them on to my daughter who has become a proficient binder to add to her hobbies. Does this prove that skills are hereditary?

Lyham Road school was and still is, typical of the standard L.C.C. school built in the late 20's / early 30's period, with large, lofty, airy rooms, I cannot remember ever feeling cold at school during the winter. My first promotion, if one can call it that, was as window boy. Some of the windows, which were about 12 feet high, had blinds fitted. It was my job to open or shut the windows or lower or raise the blinds as required by the teacher. The next step was to Class Prefect and then House Prefect, which I attained, in my last year at school. A requirement of being a prefect was that one had to make their own badges. This was from a piece of sheet copper about ½" high x 2" long, the piece was covered with wax, then carefully scratched through the wax with the word 'PREFECT', then with a pipette, acid was dropped into the scratched word to etch the word into the copper. Then the whole was highly polished.

Of course we were carefully supervised by the school Lab' teacher when this was being done.

The classes were large in pre WW2 days, up to 45 and sometimes more. We were taught the elements very early, the arithmetic tables, good writing, and above all the ability to read and to assimilate what we read. Among our teachers great emphasis was placed on teaching us to read and spell correctly and quite rightly they took the view that without the ability to read one could never learn.

Teachers served we children well during the 30's, despite the large classes. We had discipline, consideration, care, and above all persistence from our teachers to ensure that what they were teaching we learned.

In 1938 our Lyham Road school was given a new name, that of

'Parkside', As far as I could trace the name Lyham Road back, there never was a park near the school. It remains a mystery, probably a whim of the L.C.C. We were lucky to have had a large swimming pool on the premises; other schools in the locality shared this.

I was never able to swim and still cannot float, even when in the Royal Navy during WW2, I was sent to the Naval swimming school to learn after two weeks I was returned to my unit with my records stamped 'Not fit for sub-mariner duties'. I suppose if we were all supposed to be able to swim we would have had fins on our feet, or perhaps we would have all been sub-mariners. Ironically during the war I circumnavigated the world, and even when serving on Aircraft Carriers, which were very prone to enemy attack, I was never concerned that I couldn't swim, I felt that if I were to be 'Dropped into the drink' I would survive in some fashion. Well it is still yet to be proved, and I may be too old now to test the theory, I hope.

PRANKS AND GAMES

At the top of Lyham Road there was a Carter Patterson depot, which was opposite my school, Carter Patterson were one of the largest parcel carriers in London before WW2, they had many depots.

A typical soapbox with ball bearing wheels

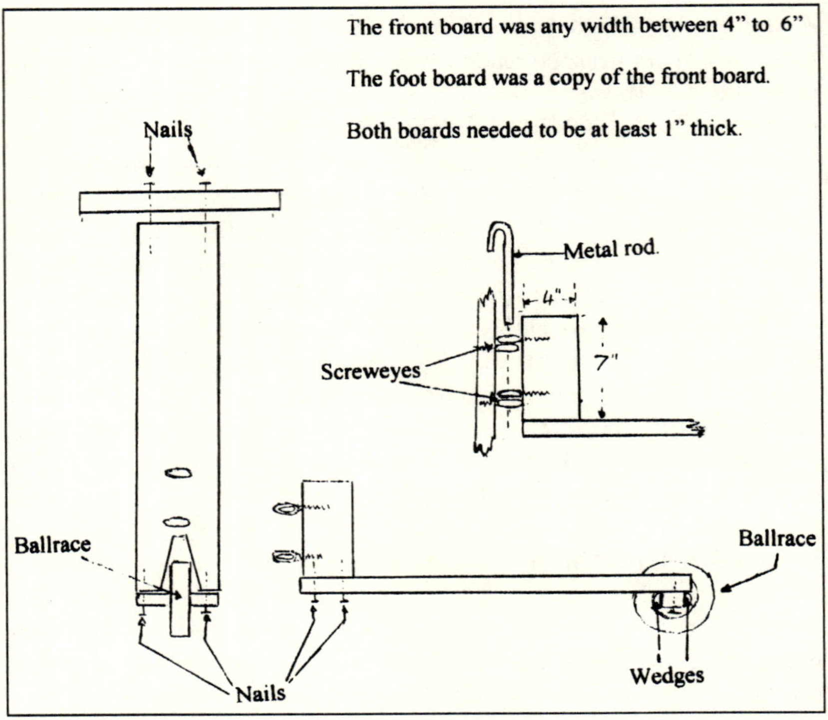
The front board was any width between 4" to 6"
The foot board was a copy of the front board.
Both boards needed to be at least 1" thick.
Nails
Metal rod.
4"
7"
Screweyes
Ballrace
Ballrace
Nails
Wedges

My scooter circa 1939

This Brixton depot still had some horse drawn carts and some late 20's solid tyred Albion vans, I still have one of the radiator badges that came from one of the vans that was involved in an accident, in Acre Lane, in 1935. This is a beautiful piece of pre war enamel work, that one does not see on modern vehicles.

One favourite pass time was to wait at the King's Avenue end of Lyham Road with our soapboxes; Lyham Road is about one mile long, and straight, with a downhill run. The object was to hitch a ride at the back of the Albions, these had a wide low step at the rear, and it was easy to jump on the step when the van was moving. The vans would only do 20m.p.h. on a flat road, on the hill the speed dropped to about 12m.p.h. Two of us would ride to the top of the hill pulling our soap box cart behind us, and just as the van turned into the depot we would jump off and coast all the way down to where we started, great harmless fun.

The other street gangs tried to muscle in on our fun, but we had the advantage as we were at the start of the road where it joins Kings Avenue. This lasted until 1939, when in that year the old vans were replaced by much faster vehicles without a step at the back, and so that joy in our lives died.

Sometimes we would hitch a ride behind a horse cart, if any one saw us the cry of "whip behind guv'nor" would go up, the cart drivers could sometimes reach behind with their long whip. More often than not the driver would climb down and walk behind and chase us off, then he would walk faster to catch up with his cart and horse which had just plodded on.

When we graduated on to scooters I became good at making these. Uncle Jim had some time before given me a few tools; I had a small saw, a hammer, and a worn out pair of pliers. I also had a tin box in which I kept any nails and screws and anything useful that I found. I scrounged wood for the scooters from the wood merchant in Acre Lane

He was only too pleased to lessen the pile of old wood in his yard, I was always grateful whenever I found a piece that had been planed smooth. The wheels were old commercial vehicle hub ball bearings, usually about 4 to 6 inches in diameter, the bottom and front were two pieces of wood, each 26"x 1"x 2". A block was needed about 4"x 4"x 6", some odd pieces of 1"x 1" wood, also required was 4 large screw eyes and a 7" bolt and nut. My source of bearings was from a friend of my father who was a foreman mechanic at Escotts in Acre Lane, a company which serviced large vehicles. I popped down there whenever I needed bearings, he allowed me to select what I wanted from a large bin of discarded bearings. I favoured a larger one at the rear; it gave a bigger surface to stamp on when there was a need to lock up the rear wheel, for maximum braking power. There was no doubt of the speed we ran at when coming down Lyham Road.

At one time it was a craze, it lasted about two years when everyone had one, there was always some one in the yard helping me to build a scooter, I always had a good stock of bearings, some were bartered for other items such as stamps for my collection.

With our scooters, we were the devils of the neighbourhood, because of the noise we made. The pavements were surfaced with slabs of York stone which gave a very good grip to the steel wheels, these slabs had been there since1890, when the road was laid out. Of course they were well worn, and because of the rising cost of natural stone they were being replaced with concrete slabs, the new slabs gave poor grip for skates and were not popular. They also increased the noise level, we all thought it was a plot to stop us skating. The old slabs were easily sold to the Garden nurseryman's businesses, now called Garden Centres. The old slabs were ripped up wholesale and soon disappeared forever.

All scooters were banned from school, one teacher had a particular dislike for them, he thought I was the ringleader for the whole confounded noise that went on after school hours. He was always preaching quietness and tranquillity, his son had a normal scooter with rubber wheels, which we all thought was rather sissy. For a bit of fun we built the schoolmaster's son a scooter, knowing full well that his father would go berserk, as he surely did, he broke it up on the spot, we never heard the last of it. I never got my bearings back. The lad was never a member of our gang, and when he gazed on us from afar I suspect he longed to join us, his father made sure he didn't. They moved away shortly afterwards, I often wondered where they went.

We held races in the square, because of the few motor vehicles that used the square the road was quite safe to use as a playground, tracks were marked out in chalk, with turning circles at each end. We appointed non-skaters as marshals to make sure that racers kept to the track, each street of those that ran off Lyham Road had their champion, and champions raced champions. Although I was never a champion, our square was champion more times than any other street. Happy halcyon days.

After scooters and in the years leading up to the outbreak of war, we became proficient skaters; we all started off with cheap Woolworth skates and the graduated to better quality skates from Halfords who had a large shop opposite Lambeth Town Hall. They sold a whole range of skates from 5/- (25p) a pair up to £1.1.0 (£1.5p) a pair, I bought my first ball bearing wheeled skates from them costing 7/6d (37½ p).

Skating was an improvement over scooters, there was less maintenance needed, on the scooters the screw eyes were always pulling out of the block, at least with skates one could always buy new wheels when the old ones wore out. They were 1/- (5p) each. The old stone slabs were wonderful to skate upon, but like scooters, on the concrete slabs one had to be careful. Strathleven Road was a wonderful place to skate, the whole of the left-hand side going away from Acre Lane was unbroken, with no intersections.

We became expert skaters, able to do all sorts of things, jumping, spinning, sitting down on one skate, and dancing. The secret of good skating was a good stout pair of shoes. The skates were fixed to the shoe by means of a screw pulling together two clamps, one on each side of the sole, then there was an ankle strap, many a street skater came to grief when a skate pulled the sole off the shoe. Uncle Jim fixed mine by using steel caps from a pair of working clogs riveted to my skates, the toes of my shoes simply slid into the caps a good tight fit.

Our first skates were primitive, just a sole plate mounted on four axles, with the wheels held on by a split pin. Later, modern skates arrived from America; these were the first steerable skates. These had wide steel ball bearing wheels that were retained by a lock washer and a nut, these also had rubber blocks between the axles and the sole plate, by leaning to one side or the other they could be steered. Then immediately before the war, wide hard rubber wheels were available. This immediately took away the main cause of complaint, the noise. But raised another complaint, this of approaching old people without any warning and frightening them, our youthful days were full of grownups grumbling about us, but at least we had a youth to remember, not like the youth of today, if there is such a thing.

During the school holidays one year we thought we would skate to Brighton, this being the nearest seaside to Brixton, we worked out a time based on our knowledge that once we got a rhythm going we could maintain 10 miles an hour. We decided to take the tram to Purley terminus, this would save us 15 miles, we duly arrived, had a meal of fish and chips, pitched the tent and settled down for the evening on the beach.

We lay there chatting away, when some called out and told us to move our tent to underneath the main pier because where we were would be swamped when the tide came in. The next morning we packed up and realised our skates would not carry us back to Brixton, and what's more neither would our legs and ankles, the wheels were badly worn and our body bits were badly swollen. This was crisis time, what to do now, after a count there was not enough for one train fare home, let alone four more, we couldn't telephone because no one had a phone in the house, finally someone said suggested going to the Police station, and so we did. The constable at the desk wouldn't believe our story until he saw the state our skates were in and our legs convinced him to have a word with his sergeant. He took our names and addresses and assured us that we had done the right thing, he then told us to wait. After a while a man in Salvation Army uniform came into the waiting room, and told us that he was going to put us on a train at Brighton station which would take us to Clapham Junction station. Then another man would meet us a make sure that we got home safely. He duly put us on the train and away we went. What an adventure to go home by train, we were met as arranged and the new man took us by tram to Clapham. He walked with us to our homes and told our parents the story, and that the cost would be 3/6d each for train and tram fares plus phone calls to London, he left an address where to send a postal order for that amount. As he left each house he gave each of us a good ticking off for being so foolish, phew! That evening father went berserk, hollering and shouting until Uncle Jim came up the stairs to find out what was going on. Father told him that 3/6d was a night in the pub for him, Uncle Jim said "Here pay it out of this, and give the boy the change", he then put two halfcrowns on the table and left us.

Needless to say I never did broach the subject of the change. Such days, naughty, yes, but never criminal, but such fun.

Skates were taboo for a few weeks, and in any case we had to raise some money to pay for new wheels.

There was always a need to earn pocket money, the best way we ever found was our firewood business, four of us worked together collecting and cutting the wood, then each pair of us had our round to do, on Sundays the money was put together and split four ways. We made a variation of the soap box carts, but these were six feet long, these were towed down to Brixton market on Friday and Saturday nights. There we collected wooden boxes of any kind from the stalls; the reader must bear in mind that these markets were open until midnight on Saturdays. The stall holders were glad to have the boxes cleared a couple of times during the evenings, sometimes we were paid a couple of 'tanners' for our trouble. We never made less than six runs a night

The boxes were fruit and green vegetables mostly, from the butcher stalls we collected egg cases and bacon boxes, these were loaded on to our carts and stacked as high as we could reach, a couple of ropes aver the top pulled tight, and away we would go. 'Nigger', one of the lads lived on the corner of Ellerslie Square and Lyham Road; his house had a large back yard with a lean to shed. All the boxes were stacked in the yard and the first job was to flatten them and put them under cover to keep the wood dry. All day Sunday we cut the wood up and tied it into 1lb bundles ready for sale. Monday to Thursday according to our needs, we hired costermonger barrows from Jones the greengrocer for 6d an hour. We had a set of scales for each barrow which we had bought second hand in case any customer wished to check the weight of any bundle, we were never challenged. The wood sold for 2d a bundle, in a good week we could make 30/- (£1.50p) each. We kept this up with our other jobs, the paper rounds and the battery rounds and each week we did very well. There was money to be had if one was prepared to work for it; this was the situation up to the outbreak of war in 1939.

We gave up the firewood caper when the war started, had we known that there would be a false period we could have gone on for a few months more, however, others, realising how well we had done started up in competition, so it was just as well we finished when we did. As the war went on the supply of boxes dried up because of no fruit coming into the country. Wood was still available from Ironmongers, it was not popular because it was invariably wet and needed drying. A quirk of war however suddenly made a source of wood available as firewood, it was timber from bomb shattered houses.

The last memory of collecting the boxes was of cold nights, during such winter evenings we would buy a penny bag of roasted chestnuts or a hot potato. To stand near the stove was a chance to thaw out. The chestnut man can still be seen, albeit rarely, but the potato man has alas, gone forever.

There were many pranks we played on the miserable grown up's. Ellerslie Square houses, were for some reason unknown, divided by two rows of railings, from the front doors to the pavement, these rails were about six inches apart, on dustbin collection days, most people put their bins out on the doorstep, the night before. If one of the 'grumps', as we called them, had complained about the noise we made when playing in the street, we would creep to their door and lift the full dustbin to balance on the narrow railings, then a piece of string would be tied from the dustbin handle to the front door knob. A sharp 'rat-tat' on the door, the poor inmate would open the door and the dustbin would tip up and empty itself on the doorstep. It was a case of, they didn't like us, and we didn't like them.

Another prank at night was to tie two knockers together with black string and a piece of elastic, a knock on the door would bring the inmate to the door, and as the door opened it would raise the next door knocker. The first door would be shut because no one was there, and this would cause the other knocker to bang down. If we were lucky it would repeat itself. The funniest thing was that the 'grumps' would get used to a knock with no one there and would not bother to answer, when someone knocked on the door and was a genuine visitor, they would knock and knock on the door and never get an answer.

There was a small United Dairies shop in Acre Lane, next door to 'The Hope & Anchor'; the manager was a most miserable man who appeared to dislike all schoolboys. Some of us had a paper round with Hunter's, the newsagents next door to the dairy shop. The miserable manager would not even stand for us to be outside Hunters; his usual cry was "Clear off". Outside his dairy there was two large bins full of eggs, 1/- a dozen fresh laid, or 6d a dozen for cracked eggs. The manager was so obnoxious that some of the lads decided to get their own back, (not our pals of course.), they simply skated past at speed and as they passed they dropped a large stone in the fresh egg bin. So fresh eggs became cracked eggs. He was transferred soon afterwards, and was replaced by a local lady who knew us, she was quite pleasant.

I suppose if war had not intervened, we may have grown up like some of today's youth, being more than just naughty, I think war brought out the best in all of us, we were so occupied in condensing ten years growing up into two.

RELIGIOUS THOUGHTS

We lads had a good source of scrumping, it was in Rodenhurst Road, and it was the back garden of a big house that was used by a religious sect called 'Elim Tabernacle'. We found a way in, I suppose I should say; we made a way in, through the fence of the house next door. We didn't take a lot of fruit, we just stuffed our jerseys with apples and pears until we looked like pregnant pigs. We got caught one day by one of the occupants who said we were stealing God's fruit, the names he called us, and he being a religious man, most ungodly.

Talking of religion. At one time I joined the Boy's Brigade, after a few weeks I realised it was not for me. I was undecided what to do, mother wanted me to stay with them, as it would keep me out of mischief, but father thought "It was a bloody daft thing to be in anyway", Uncle Jim said "Do what you feel is right boy". Armed with this wealth of knowledge I left. On the last Sunday I attended, it was a special Baptism service. I saw a girl just one or two years older than myself; she was dressed all in white and entered the water until fully immersed. As she rose, I was overcome with a tremendous sense of well being and peace, a sense of being uplifted to some other, much more serene place. After the ceremony was over I was troubled for weeks. I left the brigade still with the problem, which eventually faded.

I think that is the nearest I ever got to being called to the church, I was nearly fourteen then, seventy eight now, and I have never had that feeling since, I sometimes wonder why or even if it would be possible, perhaps it is not too late yet. What do people who have the call obtain that I cannot, it is said that God moves in mysterious ways, with all the bombing during the Blitz and during my war service in the Pacific area, I never looked to God for salvation. The great faith that I do have and always have had is in myself. I am my own god. I always do what I think is right and proper.

Years later I was fortunate to have had a cruise to Israel. I visited Jerusalem and walked the Via Dolorosa and the steps of the cross. It was a truly moving experience and included Nazareth, Capernaum and Bethlehem. I chose that holiday deliberately to try to recapture my experience of my youth; it was not to be. Today I am still perplexed by the whole question of religion. It is incomprehensible with so many imponderables to consider, I can believe that Christ existed, but not God, do not ask me why, I just do not know, and yet I am sure I am a Christian, somewhere, somehow.

Here I am talking of a time outside the scope of this book. So, back to my youth.

OUR GANG

We were a close knit group of children who all went to the same school, which was an L.C.C. school with the posh name of 'Parkside'.

The school is still situated in Lyham road, Brixton. It was near enough to enable most of us to go home for the mid-day meal. When the bell to return tolled I could just make it if I ran all the way.

There were twelve of us who played regularly together in the same square (Ellerslie Square.), there were two Ronnie's, two Billy's, Nig, Doreen, Frankie, Jacky, Alec, Chris, and Vera (my future first wife.), Vera always seemed to be taking peoples babies for walks in prams.

A gang in our school days is not as gangs are today, it was a group of children who stayed together thoughtout school life, each road had it's own gang. The next Road to Ellerslie Square was Kildoran Road; this didn't have a gang because very few children lived there. Then in ascending order going up Lyham Road were Margate Road, Mauleverer Road and Mandrell Road, the latter had a small gang owing to only having one side with houses. Next to the houses was Carter Patterson the Hauliers, and opposite was our school. The three gangs got on well together but never joined in playful activities, they all kept to their own area's, and above all they never fought each other.

I suppose our gang was together from 1935 up to 1942. We seldom got into serious trouble (apart from the gun incident, more of this later); we were, looking back, a confounded nuisance to the folk of the Square, if only for the noise we made.

I can only remember one spot of real damage we caused. This was when a local builder was working in the square; all the gangs universally disliked him. He would not allow any youngster to pass by his barrow without a "Clear off". He was a real misery martin. We decided to play a prank on him one day. When he went off for his dinner at the local Pub' we left one of the lads on 'ticky' in case he came back quickly. The rest of us ran to his barrow and found it full of sand, it was a typical builders barrow, Two large wheels about 4 feet in diameter with low sides a long bar from the middle with a cross bar at the end to push or pull. We intended to push it down the Square to Burmans yard just to hide it. It was on the pavement and off we went four of us. Half way down it all went wrong, as did most of our plans, the wheel hub cap got too near to the railings of one house and snapped all the railings off at the base, being cast iron they wouldn't bend, just snapped with the sound of a machine gun. We all fled and hid. The landlord's agent visited all our parents and in due course summonses arrived for us to appear at the Balham Juvenile Court.

A few days later there was much activity in the Square and we all stood in the road and watched the Council workmen cutting down the railings and taking them away, this was part of the war effort for scrap metal. Some time later we had notices to say that the summons were withdrawn but would stay on file, who cared about that, we hadn't been tried or found guilty, and in any case later the entire Square was badly bombed and half of it was demolished. Was it fate? No it was the gang being lucky once more.

All in all the years were good years, years in which we grew up, rather independent, a little anti-discipline, always up to something or other, but above all we were really good pals.

The out break of war did not affect us as much as our elders, probably because they still had vivid memories of WW1, this had finished only 21 years before, they remembered the causalities and the men who never came back, they were right to be so concerned of course.

All the gang was suddenly to grow up before our time. All of us survived the war and we became in experience, middle aged people in their 20's.

GIRLS

The girls we played with were considered, as in our gang, most of the boys did not have much interest in the opposite sex. As we became older, we each had our girl who we asked to go out with. It was all immature as we changed from boy to girl and girl to boy, I was never much interested in girls, I seemed to feel that girls and boys who had other interests were not interested in discovering sex. In those far off days there was just not the interest that applies today, society was not as permissible as today. Nevertheless we tended to pair off and go for walks around the local streets; we all had our favourite places to go to. Sometimes two pairs would go together, there was usually some mild petting and kissing, not much more, Of course each gang had it's Casanova, who boasted of his conquests of various girls. He was usually the tear away type; we had such a lad, who was not really liked by the rest.

I had a girl for the last year before the war, we were fond of each other but nothing happened that should not have happened, she was evacuated to Devon with her school and that was the end of that.

The 'going out' with each other, was always a secretive affair, usually a lad took a shine to another lad's girl, then the girl had to tell her current boy she wanted to break it off, She then took up with the new boy and so it went on.

Things were shared, sweets, the cinema, bags of chips and just standing on the corner of the Square talking of sweet nothings, no thought or even care of the future, just the bind of school tomorrow until school finished, then joy of joy's boy meets girl again.

In those days of course, when a boy asked a girl to the cinema, he paid for the tickets and fares home, and also for a box of chocolates, and if the occasion demanded, such as a birthday, a flower to pin on her dress. Not like today where all is equal, or is it?

Vera, my future first wife, had her boy and after the gang drifted apart we met up again about 3years later, apart from war service we never were apart, she died in 1995.

She was really an outsider to the Square; the way she came into the group was really because of the Square itself. Her father had a row of lockup garages and a large yard that used to be a stable yard; these were situated in a corner of the Square.

The entrance of the yard and lock-ups was through double gates at the end of a short alley, just past a shop and it's house, the shop keeper was run by a strange man named Batty, it was a small general store that served just the Square. Through the gates there was a sharp right turn into the yard, there were nine lock-ups, Vera's father had the two largest opposite the gates, years later I had the third for my first motor-cycle and later for my first car.

Vera was often around the Square with her father when he was servicing his two vans and his car, usually on Saturdays, she got to know us and gradually became one of us.

We became engaged in 1943 when I was called up into the Royal Navy for my war service, and we married in 1947, we were together for the next 52 years, until her death at the age of 70. I am sure that Vera and I were the only pair to keep together through time, I know not of the whereabouts of the others, it seems so far away now.

Wherever they went and whatever happened to them they are all forever part of my best memories.

CHAPTER 7

AFTER SCHOOL – OUTBREAK OF WAR – A JOB – VAN GUARD

DELIVERIES IN THE BLITZ – THE BOMBING AND SOME THOUGHTS ON SOME MEMORIES

GETTING TO WORK

AFTER SCHOOL

In July 1939, mother was informed that I had won a scholarship to a Grammar school at Tulse Hill, Brixton, war was in the offing and there was talk of evacuating schools to areas away from towns and cities. Uncle Jim had bought me a new cap and blazer for the new school. I was due to start at the new school on the 4th of September 1939, the day after war was declared. I duly got myself ready and cycled to school, proud as Punch in my new outfit. The scholarship came as a gift from heaven for me, I had not looked forward to starting work at 14, and I was dead set at some time in the future in gaining a Matriculation. Now I had my chance. I arrived at the school to find a string of busses and coaches, I found someone in charge and was told to take a form home for my parents to sign, and to come back the next morning with the necessary requirements for evacuation, and without my bike. Mother would not sign the form without talking to father, after I had gone to bed I heard them arguing about it. Next morning I was told that they had decided to keep me at home because they thought that if we were going to be bombed, it would be better for us to be killed together. Good bye to my better education, Uncle Jim was very disappointed at their attitude, but they wouldn't budge. This was a widespread belief among the populations of large towns. Being bombed when they could have been saved had they gone to the country, killed hundreds of children. Based on what my father had said, I was certainly sure that I would be dead very soon. So, what now, what lay ahead? Meeting up with the gang it appeared that their parents thought the same as mine, so most of us would still be together. Because of the lack of teachers, most of whom had gone with their pupils to evacuation, the schools soon closed.

As I was the youngest, it was obvious that we would have to find work as we were all over 14 years old. But first there was the question of obtaining a gas mask, we had to report to a closed down greengrocers shop at the top of Lyham Road, people were queuing along the pavement and in about a half hour queue we came away with a gas mask in a nice cardboard box fitted with a piece of string, this was threaded through the box to enable it to be carried over the shoulder.

The wide boys soon found a way to make money, replacement gas mask boxes soon came onto the markets, these were made from all sorts of materials an in all shades of colour. We soon replaced the string with something more substantial. within a few weeks the box's became a reciprocal for all kinds of goodies, from cigarette cards to conkers. Our box's were to be seen stuck together with sticky brown paper, even sticking plasters. There was a stupid regulation that forbade the issue of a new box.

Naturally, everyone carried the gasmasks for the first few weeks and they were mislaid by the thousands, everywhere, in busses, in trams and trains, pubs, anywhere where people went.

During the phoney war people left them at home, but as soon as the bombing started, out they came again.

OUTBREAK OF WAR

I knew of course that Chamberlain had gone to Munich to see Hitler and that we had been given breathing space, on Saturday the 2nd of

An Apprenticeship to Life

September 1939 every one was talking of the war situation, my father was expecting war to be declared anyday soon.

I went out on my usual paper round, it being Sunday the third, I was with Billy, my pal at the top end of Kings Avenue, he was collecting the paper money, and I was delivering the papers. We were both unaware that war had been declared almost that minute, seven minutes later, the first air raid warning sounded. This, I thought, as probably most Londoners did at that moment, was it. Well I had enjoyed life up to that moment that this war lark had started; Billy put his gas mask on and promptly scampered back to Hunters the newsagent. This was a half-mile run and Billy being very tubby, and having his mask on, was not in a fit state to talk after having run back non stop. He promptly fled home, scared out of his wits. I went home and finished the round after lunch. I had started to run after Billy but it occurred to me, that 'Jerry' could not kill all of us in one go, so I decided to walk

Arriving home I found that my parents had been discussing the war and what to do. They had come to the conclusion that the best place to die was sitting in their favourite pub', with preferably a glass of their usual tipple, Guinness, in their hands.

I found a couple of the gang in the Square; we wondered where was the best place to go to see the action, Clapham Common? Or Stockwell Park, someone said the 'planes would not drop bombs on grass, little did we know, when bombing became indiscriminate how many bombs were to be dropped on grass. With this thought we decided to stay in the Square, after all this is where the excitement usually happened any way. All our schooling and exams were forgotten and now of no importance to us, how wrong we were to think that. We talked of what forces we would join, the Army, the Navy or the Air Force, we all plumped for the RAF I suppose we were carried away with our boyish dreams, after all we were only 14 and we had another 4 years to grow up before we would be called up into the forces. Anyway we dreamed on until the all clear sounded, the first of many hundreds we were to hear.

The warning had been nothing more than a lone French plane meandering along the channel and had turned unexpectedly toward the English coast, action never came, and so the phoney war as it was to be called, started. While we were dreaming, little did our dreams include the fear of the unknown, the air raids that were to become part of our most impressive years, the growing up years. We could not possibly dream that we were to become so hard and indifferent to the nightly raids that were to bring death and destruction all around us. So indifferent to the incendiary bombs, but how skilled we were to become at extinguishing them when they fell in their thousands, and above all how we became adept at sleeping through the noise of gun barrages and exploding bombs.

Before we were 16 each of us were to play our part in trying to save this London of ours. During the early war years I had an uncanny urge to do as much as I could to ensure our London and our comfy world we lived in was preserved and the enemy beaten, this was an urge I bore through the war, even I could not explain it.

I think I may now know the answer in this way. In recent years my daughter has been researching my ancestors, she has discovered a direct line back for over 300 years, generations have lived and died either within or very near the City of London, the square mile. Most have lived within the sound of Bow bells and are true cockneys, in fact my grandfather and his family lived in a Mews that has been dead in the centre of London for centuries. The urge is of course inborn, I am a true Londoner, not an immigrant born there by chance and claiming to be a Londoner as one reads in the press and hears on the media. The line will die with me, I have no son and my brother died so tragically. There are male cousins on my paternal side, and so the name will survive, but they will not be cockneys.

So, war had come at last, evacuation had started in earnest, some 875,000 school children had been sent away, some to more danger than if they had stayed in their homes. Many died on their way to Canada when their ship was sunk by enemy action in the Atlantic Ocean. Others stayed in the country, never to return to the towns and cities with parents killed in the air raids and their homes demolished, Most of the gang peculiarly, also stayed at home. There was now no school to go to, and as I was now over 14 I had left school anyway.

A JOB

Father wanted me to go into the printing trade; I was intent in making my own way through life. Just before the outbreak of war, father had obtained work with J.Lyons & Co Ltd, as a van cleaner, he had left the printing trade as he was becoming older and he did not want to travel

An Apprenticeship to Life

into central London with war approaching. He now worked in the Acre Lane depot; this suited him enormously as it was almost next door to his favourite pub'.

I used to watch the vans arrive back in the evening at Lyons depot in Acre Lane, Brixton. I had become friendly with the garage foreman, Bill Douglas. He was a kindly person, and never seemed to mind me looking over his shoulder whenever he was servicing or repairing the vans. Bill was then about 30; he had a charming wife Georgie, who often came to the depot on Saturday mornings. It was here that Bill heard of my tales of woe, about school and evacuation, Bill suggested that there might be a vacancy for an apprentice in the workshop, and would I be interested? He told me that he had already mentioned this to my father and that he had not had a reply. I was overjoyed, obviously I had to obtain parental consent and this was not forthcoming without argument. Father still wanted me to go into the print trade, mother said it would have been better if I had been evacuated, this indeed was a change of attitude after all the arguments we had over that, anyway it was too late for that now. As young as I was I was adamant that Lyons was where I wanted to go. Mother told father that he would have to take me to see the depot manager, Mr Snazzel. He was a small dapper man. I had spoken to him a few times before. I said that Mother told father to take me, she made the decisions and father was the lamb.

After Mr Snazzel had outlined the requirements of the job, he called Bill in who was quite happy with the prospects of eventually having me with him in the garage.

I was offered the job which I took with both hands, my starting wage was 10/- a week (50p), the national Insurance stamp was 4d (about 1½p) per week, therefore I drew 9/8d (48p) per week, mother gave me back 6d (2½p) a day. With this I bought a 1d cup of tea, a 2d pie, and a 2d bar of chocolate for my lunch, I had a penny left over. Compared with the money we earned in the pre-war years, I was poor indeed. I was very grateful for the weekend shilling sometimes more, that Uncle Jim gave me for doing the few errands during the week. Bill Doug' did private jobs on cars on Saturdays, and most times I helped him, I cleaned parts and tools etc' and in so doing I was learning all the time. However the small earnings I had from Bill on Saturdays was handy indeed, all in all my pocket money wasn't too bad.

VAN GUARD

Before an apprenticeship could be commenced in the Tea Department it was a pre requisite to learn what the companies products were, and how they were distributed. The easiest way to do this was for the young lad to be put with one of the Salesman/Drivers to work as his Vanguard for a year.

I was placed with Bob Hare; he was about 60 years old and had been with Lyons many years. He was a religious person, when we left the depot each morning he would pull up and read a short piece from his bible. I always listened intently and he seemed pleased with that. I found out that he had never been satisfied with previous boys and had constantly grumbled about them. Somehow, Bob and I hit it off, nevertheless, I always worked with Bill on at least Saturday mornings, by the time the first year had passed Bill and I had got to know each other very well.

For a year I had to be taught by Bob about the contents of the van. I started off very badly; it was about the end of the second week, Friday afternoon just after lunch, at a customer's shop. A man shook hands with Bob and walked to the back of the van, I was told to climb down and Bob told me the person was a round inspector. The man climbed up to check the stock and the interior (it was my job to keep the van clean). He turned to Bob extremely angry and asked what was this, in his hand he held an orange, I said it was mine, a previous customer had given it to me when I had carried his order to his shop. Bob was told to carry on with his round but not to deliver any of the goods in our van and the customers would get their orders early next week. I was suspended forthwith and thought goodbye to my apprenticeship. After the Inspector had left us, Bob apologised for not telling me about foodstuffs in the van, especially oranges which are highly flavour contagious to tea. There came a meeting at the depot, where Bob and Mr Snazzel and the Round inspector together with an official from Cadby Hall (J.Lyons & Co Ltd's head office.) discussed the orange affair. Because of the fact that I had only been under instruction for less than two weeks the charge was dismissed, I was called in and told so and all was well.

The different kinds of tea and the varieties of packets were truly amazing. I never ceased to wonder just how little one had to buy to become a customer on the round; it was obvious to me, not yet 15, that it did not pay to have tiny amounts of tea delivered by van. On my van we carried China, Indian, Ceylon and blended teas, we also carried ground coffee, liquid coffee and cocoa's, anything other than these three products was strictly forbidden, tea was easily contaminated when stored with other goods. Tea was packaged in parcels that weighed 6lbs; the packets were in 1d ounce size, 4ounce size, 8ounce and 3lb bags. There were various prices based on the colour of the label, these were, in ascending order of quality, Yellow, mauve, blue, red, green and orange, mauve was an introduced wartime label. The 3lb bags were for commercial use and were graded L, Y and O; I cannot recall an N or S label, of course the LYONandS spell Lyons.

The little corner shops on our round were typical of the area which was the Southeast of London, this included Stepney, Walworth, Lambeth, Bermondsey and The Borough. This area was perhaps one of the poorest parts of London, and when the 'Blitz' started, one of the most heavily bombed. The people of the area were very proud and

Typical South London corner shop that survived the war

stubborn; these attributes enabled them to sustain the nightly air raids which devastated most of the area.

These small shops would order as little as 1½ lb.'s of tea and this was of mixed values. In an area where the sales of tea were mainly of the cheap Yellow label, there would be an order of a 4oz packet of expensive Orange Label. This was usually for some poor old person who had fallen on hard times, but insisted on a decent 'cuppa', despite how he or she lived. They were so proud trying to maintain the standards of a past life. Often we would find someone waiting by the van and asking could they please have a 1d packet of Yellow label, they were too proud to go into the shop and admit their poverty. Bob, being the pious man that he was, often gave them a packet and put his own 1d in his cash bag.

I often saved my dinner money by delivering to the street stall while Bob went to his lunch, officially someone should be with the van at all times, this was one rule that was sometimes ignored. After the van was parked, Bob would go off to his lunch and I would take a couple of 3lb bags of 'L' label to a nearby street stall and collect the money, these were of course regular orders. The stall keeper would give me a hot cup of tea and a cake. This occurred two or three times a week, most of the stall keepers got to know that I loved Eccles cakes, not the small ones that are about today, but those that were about 6" in diameter, a meal in themselves.

Our 'Patch' covered the old Kent Road and the small streets around the railway yards at Rolls Road, we also covered Camberwell green and the Elephant and castle areas, and this was an area of heavy bombing. The worse incident I recall was at Camberwell Green, we always stopped at the bank during the late morning, a warning had been sounded and many people had gone into the trench shelter on the Green. Bob was in the bank and I was sitting in the van, I clearly saw the lone bomber flying toward us and heard the bombs dropping, I threw myself out of the van to lay flat on the pavement. The bombs dropped on the small houses at the back of the Green; the last one however dropped directly on the Shelter on the Green. The shelter was packed and many were killed, more than those that were injured. I was unhurt as was Bob, the van was riddled with holes and the windscreen was smashed. Bob drove the van back to the depot, about 4 miles away; it was made fit for service again in about three days. The van was a 1928 Morris 1 ton with a three-speed gearbox, a real old grinder. I saw this van again in 1987 at a

Commercial Vehicle Rally, it was then 59 years old and still running, I remember the registration number vividly, it was GJ 8931.

The area we served included Bermondsey and Rotherhithe, especially the area between the Surrey Commercial Docks and the river. The area which is on the south bank is bounded on three sides by the river, Rotherhithe road follows closely the bend of the river and joins Lower Road via Redriff Street, most of the docks were contained by these roads except Greenland dock.

Among the docks are little areas of short narrow lanes running down to the dock walls, the houses were back to back, there was usually a pub to about every 500 people. There was a mission here and there, most of the houses had seen better days, but people had been born there with their families going back over many generations, they had married there and raised their families. The old people were surrounded by their kith and kin. Those who worked probably did so in the docks, although the docks worked with casual labour there was sufficient work to keep the dockers fully employed during the early part of the war.

Between Grange Road and Old Kent Road there was the Bricklayers Arms Goods depot, the feeder lines to the depot continued on toward Rotherhithe New Road but behind Rolls Road.

There were three important bridges in the area, two in Redriff Road, the first of the two was between Greenland and Canada docks, the second between Greenland and Russia docks, the third was in Rotherhithe Street, across the entrance to Surrey Basin from the river. I came to know the area very well during the year I spent with Bob as his boy; we served the area all through the bombing and the Blitz during 1940/41.

Each day as we went to our deliveries we found more and more of the area missing, yes, just that, missing. One would go back to the depot down streets where the next time we saw them had great gaps in them where houses, and sometimes our customers once stood. Our customer index book was becoming smaller each day, and our order load was becoming smaller each week.

On the night of September 7th 1940, 'Black Saturday', the entire area was saturation bombed. During the day 300 bombers had dropped their deadly load on the docks and the riverside boroughs, but the worse was to come during the same night. 247 bombers dropped 335 tons of high explosive and 440 tons of incendiary canisters; there were also a number of land mines dropped.

During the following Monday Bob and I endeavoured to maintain our deliveries, there were many incidents that had meant diversions. In many places we left the van as near as we could to the customer and carried the order up the street picking our way through the debris, even while firemen and rescue men were still working. In many cases the customers shop was either demolished or blasted.

Looking back all those years ago, it seems to me that it was a miracle that we were not hurt because we never stopped when a raid was in progress. More than once the van was rocked by bomb blast, and once, an incendiary bomb dropped directly in front of us, we ran over it and escaped.

That night, bombing was the worse that Bob and I had ever witnessed seeing the next morning. For the first time in my young life I was very grateful that I was with a man who was so confident and so self assured that no harm would become us, it was the first experience that I had in the power of a believer of God.

Many people had been made homeless and had been sent to Keetons Road School; this had been opened as a reception centre. The people were waiting for transport to safer areas, we had delivered an emergency order of tea to the school that morning, and they had to sleep another night at the school because for some reason the busses hadn't arrived. The same night during the raid a large bomb plunged directly onto the school, over 400 men, women and children died. When we were able to enter the area again we found the carnage dreadful and we had so few customers left. The area never recovered from that night.

The night of the 8th again bought carnage to the strained ARP resources,171 bombers dropped 207 tons of incendiary bombs, and each canister contained 161 Kilo-gram bombs, which were scattered layer by layer as they dropped from the aircraft. That night of the 7th/8th there were 122,720 incendiary bombs dropped.

The next day I saw ships and barges ablaze on the river, barges were adrift on the river fully loaded with blazing timber, riverside buildings were blazing for days, there was no water to put out the fires. Many shopkeepers I had grown to know and like had been killed or maimed. Some were never found, many just abandoned the area and left. It was much more sorrowful for Bob who had known these people for many years, in fact since the early 30's.

Bob was very philosophical about the bombing. He took the view that it was now, more than ever before that people needed their cup of tea. It was his job and duty to make sure that tea was available, he considered it as his war service.

For myself, the knowledge I gained each day enabled me to discuss with the adults the damage of the night before, when I returned home in the evening the first question was 'what's it been like today'. Of course, having faced the desperately damaged districts during the day, I, with tens of thousands of others, had to face the nights. In one respect I was grateful to be living in Brixton as we suffered less bombing than the dock areas, although our house was demolished and the bombers made a bit of a mess of the house we had just removed to.

In the period from September 7th 1940 until September 18th, just twelve days and nights, the bombers dropped 2,289 tons of high explosive bombs and 496,480 incendiary bombs, this does not include those dropped during daylight raids

I cannot recall ever taking cover in an air raid shelter, I always felt safer in the open, although I once had a near miss when what I thought was a piece of shrapnel coming down, I ducked, and it thumped the ground just a few feet away. It was a complete nose cap of an anti-aircraft shell, A precious acquisition to my collection, not many of them were found intact. It was probably fired from the guns on Clapham; they were 4.5's as was the nose cap. These were solid brass and weighed about 2½ lbs.

During the dog fights in daylight it was common to hear the machine gun belt links clattering onto the roof tops of houses, we lads clambered to collect them, ignoring all that was going on around us. I still believe to this, day that this foolhardy bravado stemmed from the attitude of our parents, those lads who had parents who were 'scaredy cats' as we called them, were scared themselves. I remember my father, on hearing the news of the outbreak of war, simply said "I am off to the 'Hope' to have a drink on it". I said "On what Dad", he said "On me". He then said "The buggers nearly got me last time and they are not going to do it this time". As he survived the First World War so he survived the second. That just about summed up my father's fear of war.

During the early raids there was a feeling of 'Alltogherness', all barriers of class and neighbourly differences went by the board, every one helped every one. During the False war period after the declaration, the ARP services were looked upon with some hilarity and disrespect, cartoons were drawn of them with a general sense of scorn.

When the bombing started people soon found out what an air raid warden was worth, he quickly became the authority of what to do and when. He became invaluable after an incident, when there would be people to rehouse and care for. Training was sketchy when they started but with the bombing came experience, and with experience came knowledge. It was a strange thing that people like myself, the civilians of London, had experienced the baptism of fire long before most of the British and Commonwealth armed forces.

Before Bob and I set off on our daily round we were briefed with the other salesmen and their boys in the large general office. The office was about 25' square with a work top on three sides where the salesmen made up their books at the end of the day while the boys loaded up the vans for the next day's work. The depot manager would hold a brief meeting to discuss any reports he had received of the nights bombing. The 'grape vine' was pretty accurate and the reports usually took this approach; - "Bob, Camberwell was hit last night, Mr so and so has cancelled his order, look him up if you can and let me know what's what"

Even though shopkeepers had their windows shattered or the front blown in, they still tried not to inconvenience their traders such as us and would telephone in with their instructions. I mentioned the fronts being blown in; quite often the fronts would be sucked out. Bombs were funny things; there was as much suction as there was expansion of air. It became the rule more than the exception to find nearly all our customers had their windows boarded up, glass had become hard to obtain, and in any case there was no sense to replace windows if only for them to be blown in again.

The older Victorian style shops were boarded up at the end of the working day with large shutter boards that exactly fitted the windows, these were held secure by long metal straps that were padlocked to a staple. When the 'Blitz' started slogans were painted on the boards, such as 'Our windows are gone, but we're still here'; others sometimes had a remark about Hitler's parentage.

One street stall we had on our round was sited at the back of

Camberwell Green with its back on to the green. We arrived one morning and Bob asked why had the stall been turned around, the customer said "I didn't do it, the bomb did". The building behind had been hit a couple of nights before and the blast turned the stall right round and all that was damaged was some crockery that was broken. "I am going to leave it this way" he said that the view was better for him and his customers. Some time later he had to turn it back because he had not applied for planning consent, and he could not persuade the council that he had not done it himself. Even in wartime officialdom would have its way.

Animals bombed out were very predictable, cats would keep near their old home but dogs would wander. Later when in the Home Guard I recovered many cats and took them back to the Home Guard post, at one time there were so many cats about that some wag put a sign over the door, 'The Cattery'. Many people came round and recovered their cat from our bunch. It was tragic to see old people weeks after they were bombed out still searching the rubble for a lost pet. We kept a note and description of any dead animals we found on our patrols and any nametags we found.

We once had a white Cockatoo that flew free for a while, after one bad night we didn't see it anymore.

Bob and I were delivering one morning in Albany Road, Camberwell, the siren had gone off and all was quiet. The shop we were delivering to was a butcher that had a small provision counter, they usually had about 4lb's of mixed tea a week. As we got to the back of the van the guns started up and as we looked up to the sky we saw the aircraft, then we actually saw a bomb falling. Bob dashed back into the shop and crouched between two large cold store cabinets. I ran across the road and threw myself flat on the pavement and rolled sideways into the gutter under the van. The bomb hit a house on the Butchers side of the road about 200yds away, the van rocked violently, there was a terrific bang from above. I didn't hear the explosion, but I was aware of a prolonged sound of breaking glass, I rolled out from under the van and stood up. There was dust every where, and I was covered in it. I stood up and on looking round I saw that the front kerb side windscreen and pillar was gone, Bob's raincoat and my jacket were missing and they were never found, and the big bang was a large piece of lamppost hitting the pillar. In front of the van among the debris I found a piece of bomb casing with a German 7 marked on it. I prized that piece for years. Thoughts then turned to Bob; the front of the shop was shattered. It was fortunate that Bob ran into the shop shouting to take cover, there were two women, the butcher and Bob in the shop. The butcher and the ladies had dived behind the counter which faced the window, it was a big old-fashioned counter and this saved them from flying glass. Bob had crouched between two large cold store cabinets, above, the chimneystack had collapsed through the roof and this caused a large stock of wrapping paper to crash through the ceiling directly above Bob. The cabinets took most of the weight of the paper but Bob was buried. We got him out, he had some sort of shoulder injury, and although he was in pain he insisted on driving back to the depot. The van was checked and found drivable and we drove back to Acre Lane. This was the second time that we had driven back in this fashion, out of all the vans that were based at Acre Lane only one other was put out of action and that one was garaged away somewhere in Kent. It was totally destroyed in an air raid while in a garage overnight.

Bob did not report for work the next day, he had arrived home in pain after a three hour train journey which was caused by diversions. He went to the local hospital where he was found to have a cracked collarbone and torn muscles. For the next few days I stayed in the depot and worked with Bill Douglas, without the van and Bob, I was high and dry.

An illustration of Bob's attitude to the enemy was that when he went back to the van after being released, he was clutching his pocket bible, he said to me "I mustn't think of hatred".

People just carried on no matter what the cost. For example, the woman who lived in the house that the bomb dropped on was in with her next door neighbour who had a Morrison shelter. This was a very heavy steel table, used as such at normal times, but underneath it made an excellent shelter, the two women were dug out, shocked but unhurt. All the lady of the house could think of was her cat, the cat was unhurt and was looked after by the butcher and his wife who told Bob and I the story when we called on him after his shop was temporarily repaired and reopened. The butcher also told us that the aircraft that we saw was a Messerschmidt 109 that was shot down on it's return journey to France, by a Hawker Hurricane from Tangmere.

Vera, my wife worked as a typist at the 'Bluehouse Laundry' which was situated on the corner of Kings Avenue and Clapham Park Road. During an air raid the machines were shut down and the staff made their way into the surface brick shelter, this was in the transport yard, just before a bomb dropped into the yard and exploded causing much damage to the laundry sufficient to shut the works down permanently. The end of the shelter was demolished, yet remarkably no one was even injured except for a couple of ladies who were rendered deaf, but recovered after a few days. This shows that bombs were so unpredictable in their effect. My wife remarked on the amount of dust that arose, this I found was a common factor that all H.E. bombs had.

THE BOMBING AND THOUGHTS ON SOME MEMORIES

Morning after morning we picked our way over bomb damage to get to our shops. There were collapsed buildings, masses of glass, the Heavy Rescue squads still digging for buried people, broken telephone lines, broken power cables, water mains broken and allowing water to run down holes where the mains should be. Often a gas main was burning with a loud roar. Streets were impassable for vehicles; there would be huge squads of men and sometimes women clearing the rubble away.

Bombed houses caused many problems, for example some owners of property were never traced or the deeds found, many deeds were burnt or destroyed in their houses, It was tragic that people who had lived in their houses for many years died among their belongings and their proof of ownership. It was as if the enemy was intent on obliterating some families completely, which indeed, in some cases is exactly what happened.

The determination that people found evolved from uncertainty and even fright, that most had in 1939 and early 1940. As soon as the bombing started in earnest the population gained a philosophical outlet, It became common place to hear that 'A bomb will not hit you unless it has your name on it' or 'You will only go when your number is up'. As young people we abandoned all thoughts of safety when we ran the streets during a raid seeking pieces of shrapnel and bomb cases. We stood in doorways waiting to hear a 'ping' as another piece hit the roadway. A quick dash to find it with a glove on one had in case the piece was too hot to hold. We swapped and bartered for the pieces, there was one glorious day during the battle of Britain, and a massive dogfight took place over Clapham. Spent cartridge cases and cartridge belt clips rained down in dozens, we made up a length of belt about 2'6" long, all British, I never heard of any of my friends being hurt by sky debris although many people were injured and some were killed.

There was a battery of 4.7" AA guns on Clapham common, when these were firing, the amount of metal that rained down was enormous, and a steel helmet was truly an asset.

I acquired a civilian type of steel helmet, workmen left it behind when they were clearing bomb debris in the Square, and I exchanged it later for an army issue when I joined the Home Guard. For falling sky debris the British helmets gave better protection than the American types without the wide brim.

We explored bombed houses and found pathetic belongings of those that had lived there, I often wondered what the people had been like, who they were what had happened to them, were they good or bad. My mother used to say, "only the good go first", in spite of her alcoholism she had many profound sayings. I often wondered if we had a right to roam around these dwellings, not legally but morally. Was I trespassing on the memories of those now gone, I pondered much on these thoughts, I am convinced that I was much clearer in thought as a boy of 14½ years as my mind was not cluttered with responsibilities of life.

I was very worried about my future, losing Grammar School niggled at the back of my mind. It seemed strange that I worried about this more than any other thing throughout the war, it was silly I suppose when 'Jerry' could have ended my life and made me another statistic.

It was incredible that night after night the old people stumbled through the blackout to meet at their local pub'. Because of the blackout, the interior of the bars became smoke filled dens, ventilation was poor because of the close fitting curtains that stopped the light from within getting out. Each bar had a system of light locks whereby the outer door had to be closed before the inner one was opened.

Many people were injured in the blackout. My mother in law, then to be, was injured when a hefty young man was running fast in the dark, he crashed into her in Acre Lane and knocked her to the ground, he said he was sorry and ran on. She was then 58 years old, she died when she was 81, her health between these years left a lot to be desired. She died of Meningitis, the Doctor said it was probably caused by a fall or a blow to the head in the past. Well, life does have some funny quirks.

We lads had a peculiar yodel type of recognition call, very high pitched, it was very useful in the blackout as it was very penetrating, I have not heard it in modern times, nor have I ever read or heard it elsewhere. I feel it is now a part of local history.

I had cause to visit that area of Brixton in 1984, I fancied I heard the call, is it still about or was it an echo of the past I heard. I tried to locate the old Square but realised it had gone, it had been demolished, vanished into the past. It is all part of a new trading estate, there is now nowhere to recall the Square, even by sight, all the secret corners were gone, forever. Yet memories are not so much of places as they are of people, it is all in ones mind, pictures of the mind, after all that is what memories are, just pictures. The sharp pictures are the best ones because they are the happy ones; the blurred ones are the unhappy ones. There is nothing to remind me of the devastation of the Square caused by the bomb that dropped on Uncle Jim's house, all I have is a newspaper clipping of the Square after it had been cleared of rubble. Some pre-fabs had been erected, and were there for a few years but even they were gone. I feel a tremendous sense of outrage that all the memories of so many people has been obliterated, started by Hitler and later perpetuated by our authorities after the war. Was anyone ever consulted if they wanted their Square vandalised by officialdom? I doubt it. Oh yes, some kind soul named the new buildings 'Ellerslie Square Industrial Estate', I am forever grateful to them.

When I come to write of the years 1943 to the present, I feel that although I experienced much more, saw much more, and did much more, none of it made as much impression as the years from 1928 to 1943 did.

GETTING TO WORK

One of the biggest problems after a night raid was getting to work. Usually there were roads and streets somewhere on the route either blocked completely or covered in rubble, worse was the areas where there was an unexploded bomb, then all the surrounding roads were closed. The Tramway's suffered most of all, once the lines were blown up trams had to stop and reverse with a lot of changing over of passengers from one car to another.

Having a bicycle was an asset, I distinctly remember cycling over glass and rubble and having very few punctures, I had formed a theory that if I ran on soft tyres I would not get punctures, I like to think it worked.

There were unfamiliar 'Diversion' signs always following an air raid after bombs had been dropped, the trouble with such signs was, that once you obeyed the sign and turned off on to another road you were on your own, there was nothing more to guide you. Buses were able to negotiate most diversions, although it was strange to see a Bus running down a narrow, mean, back street. When a bus depot was hit, as many were, the Buses just stopped running. As London's Buses numbered less and less many Provincial Towns and Cities loaned their Buses to London. It was odd to see 'Bournmouth', 'Liverpool', 'Manchester' and other places written on the side of the Buses.

Morning after morning masses of people picked their way through piles of rubble on their way to work. Sometimes to reach their destination only to find they had no work, just a ruined building, most of them set to trying to save any thing that was recoverable, especially office machines, these were unobtainable quite early in the war. Although people sometimes walked miles to work, often through an air raid, not many refused, they considered it a challenge to get there, I cannot remember ever missing a day from work due to enemy action. Many times it was late when one got there, the sole topic of conversation was how one got to work and where the bombs were dropped during the night. "I hear that Southwark got it last night", "Yes I walked through the Borough Road this morning", this was the kind of conversation that was heard each day. We kept track of the factories and places that had been hit. Sometimes a colleague was very late coming in and after lunch we began to guess that something had happen overnight to him or her or theirs.

It was quite commonplace for people who had suffered a blasting overnight to still turn up for work, there was an air of stubbornness in people, and this was totally opposite to what Hitler expected. The population became more determined instead of more frightened. This was especially so of the generation of the first World war period. Each night people carried on in the pubs as though there was no war on.

This was the picture in most of the West and Southern Boroughs of

An Apprenticeship to Life

East London, later most other boroughs suffered equally with damage injuries and death.

The East London Boroughs around the docks consisted of narrow streets of terraced cottages. These were back to back with no garden or yard that could have an Anderson shelter and of course the first massed raids were unleashed on the docks on September 7th 1940. There was no 'All clear' for the next 65 days and nights, and on each of those nights we had not less than 200 bombers flying over London. The only shelters that could be constructed for the mean houses around the docks were the surface brick built ones. These stood in the roadways, and when they were blasted they usually had many casualties and deaths, they also became street toilets and smelled decidedly unhealthy. Eventually they fell into disuse. There was panic in certain areas and masses of people fled to anywhere safe, many went to the Hop fields in Kent and simply camped out anywhere they could find shelter, this movement was condemned by the Government to prevent the panic spreading. It was the opening of the Underground stations as shelters that eased the situation, but then people refused to leave the stations at all, even during the day.

It is not my intention to write a history of the 'Blitz', this has been by much more proficient writers than I, although not from first hand experience, I am only writing what I saw and heard.

Suffice to say the situation was partly solved on the night of 14th of November 1940 when on a clear night sky no bombers were to be seen. That night London slept, and the bombing switched to other Towns and Cities.

The greatest raid of all came on the 29th of December 1940; this was the night after the depot fire, which I will describe later. This raid destroyed 164 acres of the City around St. Paul's Cathedral and heavily damaged South London, this bought some cynical satisfaction from those in the East End where their thoughts were "Let some other poor buggar have it".

This therefore was the scene each morning when Bob Hare and I tried to make our deliveries. We some how made our deliveries (If the shop was still intact) and made our sales alongside the milkman, the postman and other tradesmen who made the daily rounds, our 'motto' was 'Carry on as usual'.

CHAPTER 8

CAFÉ de PARIS – SHELTERS – BATTLE OF BRITAIN

CAFÉ DE PARIS

My brother in law, Harry Burman, was a great friend of Al Bowlley, one of the best of the pre-war singers; he was popular during the period 1936 until his death in 1941

He sang many times at the Café de Paris which was considered by many upper crust 'night owls' as one of the best spots in London. It was thought to be safe from bombing as it was underneath the Rialto cinema in Coventry Street, it was never closed during air raids.

On the night of 8th of March 1941, the dance floor was packed as usual when a lone raider crossed London and dropped a stick of bombs. One bomb passed clean through the cinema above and exploded on the stage of the club below, killing most of the band and many dancers. Al Bowlly had finished his act only minutes before and had gone up to the entrance for a breath of night air and had escaped the explosion. He missed death that night but was killed soon afterwards by a bomb that dropped in Jermyn Street. The night-club was reopened after the war but never regained its former popularity. Like many things that were popular before the war they became insignificant afterwards when people changed their minds about the values of life.

SHELTERS AND BOMBING

The shelter system was as safe as the money that one possessed, most wealthy people had elaborate shelters built in their homes or they escaped to country areas to a safer retreat.

The Anderson shelter was named after Sir John Anderson, who was

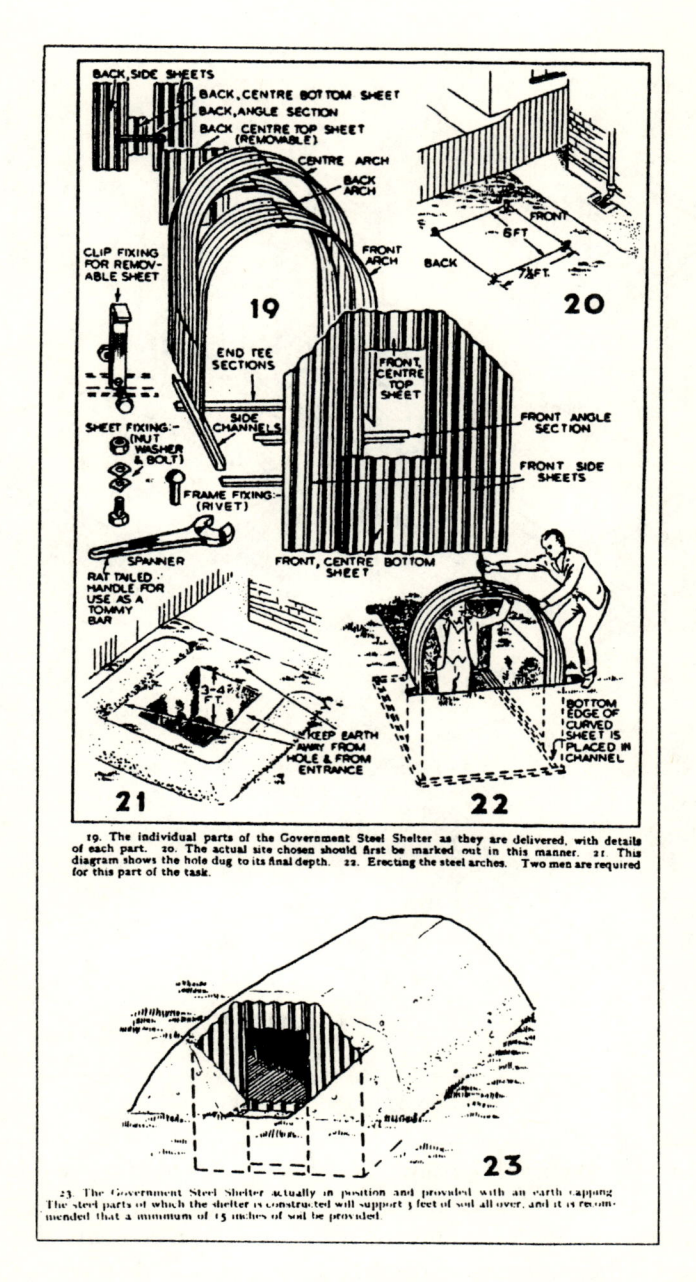

An Apprenticeship to Life

Putting up the 'Government Steel Shelter', better known as the Anderson shelter. From Modern Make and Mend, published in 1939.

How to Use the Shelter as a Table
FIGURE 8

The Morrison Shelter

---

the Home Secretary of the day. The shelter consisted of curved sheets of corrugated sheets of steel of a heavy gauge. They slept 4 or 6 people, each panel was 36" wide and about 84" high, the two curved sections bolted together at the curved ends, forming an arch, then each arch was bolted together to form a curved shelter. The ends were 84" lengths of flat corrugated steel. A hole was dug to enable the shelter to be half buried, usually in the rear gardens of houses; the soil that was excavated was piled up on top of the shelter. Half of the centre section was left open to make an entrance.

Some people who were old or infirm could apply to the local council to have the hole dug for them. Others, like my father, had to dig their own hole. He, however had other ideas, he realised that the sections laid on their sides would make a very nice chicken run. He did this and made a frame of chicken wire to cover the top. A neighbour, whose husband had been called up with the Territorials, wanted to find a home for six hens, and so we had our supply of eggs home-made. We had the hens up to the time our house was blasted. After a fruitless search we never saw our hens again.

The Anderson shelter had many abuses, they made good garages to store cars and motorcycles, they made good garden sheds and they survived for many years after the war, above all they made very good air raid shelters.

The other shelter was named the Morrison Shelter after Herbert Morrison the Minister of Production, many of the dock dwellings and other small houses had no gardens so the Morrison was an ideal substitute, albeit in a small room it was rather large, being 6'x 4'in area. The table was intended be used as a table by day and as a bed at night. This shelter saved many lives, its main faults were that if a house collapsed upon it some people suffocated from escapes of gas before they were rescued and others were drowned when the shelter was in a flooded basement.

Like the Anderson, these shelters lasted well into post war years and made excellent benches, I remember using one as an engine repair bench as late as 1964.

Over 50% of Londoners had a Morrison or an Anderson shelter delivered compared with only 2% who used the deep shelters.

The Surface shelter was not liked by most people; some of these shelters were adopted as Wardens Posts. They were constructed from poor brickwork, although this probably the best available at the time, the roof was of heavily reinforced concrete and was the greatest danger of the design. When they were subjected to heavy blast, the walls collapsed and the roof fell intact onto the rubble and the shelterers inside. These shelters became somewhere to duck into when a raid became rather 'hot'. They became dirty and damp places and were used

The Balham Tube Disaster 15th October 1940 08:00pm.
I drove along this road only a few minutes before.

An Apprenticeship to Life

Bus in Balham High Road

as convenient public toilets. Surprisingly they lasted long after the war finished.

When the bombing became intense, especially over the dock areas, people sought safer shelters than those described above; they started to use the deep tube shelters. They began to sleep on the platforms, this was initially dangerous for two reasons, and the first was they left little room for passengers to board or alight from the trains. Secondly was, because of the very crowded conditions there was a danger that people would fall onto the live rails. Eventually officialdom had to give way and allow the practise; it was common for quite small children to be sent down to the platforms to 'claim' patches for the family to sleep upon. As time went on concerts and other forms of entertainment was arranged. The biggest problem was of toilets; it started with just buckets being used with only a curtain for privacy. Then with two hundred or more sleeping on a platform people started pouring the contents of the buckets over the edge of the platforms, the stench became appalling and only ceased when chemical latrines were installed.

People started to live on the platforms permanently, there was a definite fear of health problems arising, and it was not so safe when three occurrences happened quite near to each other, these were warnings. On the night of 14th of August 1941 a bomb dropped on the main road over Balham Underground station, a large water main was broken and many people drowned. Another bomb burst through the roadway at the Bank station in the City, the blast blew many people into the path of an oncoming train, those who were not killed by the train were electrocuted when they fell on to the track. The explosion caused the largest crater ever seen in London. A bridge was built over the hole to connect the roadway and remained there until after the war, 111 people were killed in this incident.

The greatest death toll was in an East End station when people panicked when descending the stairs to the platforms. A mother with a baby in her arms and carrying bedding tripped and fell, somehow she and the child survived, but hundreds coming down the stairs also fell, crushed by others pushing in from the street, over 250 died that day. For all this it only caused a slight falling off among the shelterers. The tragedies were soon forgotten.

I scorned shelters, but always wore my tin helmet when in the street if there was a raid on. I had gained a better helmet now; this was the issue I had from the ARP, more about this later. I repeat again, a helmet was essential, the amount of rubbish that fell from the sky when a raid was on was enormous, shrapnel pinged on the pavement and roads, houses suffered broken slates by the thousands, those houses that were intact of course.

The largest area of devastation was the City of London, this was caused by the firestorm on the night of 29th December 1940, the last raid of this phase was on 10th May 1940, and it was also the heaviest. That night 1,450 people were killed. Westminster Abbey, the Tower of London, and the House of Commons were all hit.

Between September 1940 (the end of the Battle of Britain) and May 1941, just 8 months, in the London area there were 90,000 casualties, of these 20,000 died and there were 25,000 seriously injured. In the whole of Great Britain, during this period, 43,000 died, nearly half of these had lived in London. One Londoner in 6 was made homeless, this was 1.4 million people, in the borough of Stepney 4 out of every 10 houses were destroyed and many people disappeared, never to be found.

After living and working and helping throughout that 8 months, all my service for the rest of the war seemed calm by comparison.

THE BATTLE OF BRITAIN

Occasionally during the battle of Britain period, a few of the gang and myself would equip ourselves with the bell tent, sleeping bags and our cooking gear and food. The aim was to stay at Kenley airfield for the weekend. The climax of our visits to Kenley started on Friday the 16th of August. The first part of the journey was on a tram, which we boarded from Lambeth Town Hall at Brixton, after stuffing our gear under the stairs we stayed on the tram until it reached the terminus at Purley, 7 miles from Brixton. From Purley we had quite a long walk along the Brighton Road, then up Old Lodge lane which is off to the right. This led to the high ground on Kenley Common where the airfield was situated. This was the easiest airfield to get to, Croydon was nearer but it was so built up that there was nowhere with a good view.

Our aim on these trips was to see as much of our Air force and the fighter 'planes as possible, the lane that would have brought us even nearer was barricaded, this was Hayes lane.

We pitched our tent on the north side of the Airfield, there were six dispersal sites just the other side of the perimeter fence and some unusual equipment that we had not seen before. Unbeknown to us this weekend would soon reveal what use this equipment had.

We were always a bit disappointed in that Kenley was a base for 615 Squadron which had Hawker Hurricane Mk 1's. What a joy it was when we were told that 64 Squadron with Spitfire Mk 1's was also based at Kenley. I said told, we were just that, during our weekends we had become familiar to the perimeter guard patrols and one of them told us. Should he have done so? I think not, nevertheless as the wartime posters said 'Even the walls have ears'.

So to us boys that Saturday the 17th to see the 'Hurries' and 'Spits' was again a wonderful sight. We kept notes of the serial numbers of all the 'planes, sometimes we saw a strange aircraft either landing or taking off, then out came our spotter books and we argued as to what it was. We waved to all of the aircraft that took off and often we got a wave back

We never got a wave when a 'plane was landing, we guessed, rightly, that the pilot had to concentrate on what he was doing. We thought how invincible we were with our 'planes all around us. How very wrong we nearly were the next day.

We always camped near a large house called 'Highleigh' who's occupants once called for the Police to investigate us, we had a visit from a constable who was satisfied, in any case we were on common land.

Sunday dawned, we boiled the kettle for breakfast, on went the frying pan, and with eggs (which we bought from a local small holding), fried bread and bacon, and we each had a good meal, which was our main meal of the day.

The weather the day before had been hazy and cloudy, this Sunday morning looked promising but turned rather cloudy about 10.30 a.m. but it stayed dry. We cleared away after breakfast and sat around chatting and watching the odd aircraft come and go. We were thinking about lunch and arguing who would cook, when suddenly the two squadrons were scrambled, we knew then that something was up, all thoughts of lunch were forgotten. We heard the airfield siren give a warning; we had never heard this before. At twenty past one (later I found out that it was exactly 1.22 p.m.) there was a terrific roar as several German bombers came over the airfield at virtually hanger roof height and dropped their bombs. Our own guns were all firing and the noise was indescribable, one bomber was on fire. Suddenly we saw rockets go up from the strange equipment, now we knew what they were for. The rockets carried a cable which had a parachute at the top, this was fired in the path of the aircraft which if it caught the wire pulled out another parachute with the result that the Drag caused the aircraft to crash.

The bomber that was on fire caught one of the cables, the aircraft crashed in the grounds of 'Highleigh' where it burnt away. We were all laying flat and too scared to stand because of the bullets exploding in the fire, they were whizzing every where All the crew of the bomber died, The pilot was Feldwebel Peterson, his navigator Oberleutnant Ahrends. There was a passenger on board, Oberst Somers who had joined the 'plane as an official reporter to write of the attack on England and his experiences, so he gained the final experience, that of dying.

We saw bombs bouncing along the runway without exploding, a frightening sight. When the bombers had gone with our fighters hard on their heels, we looked up and high in the sky and saw another mass of aircraft in layers with what looked like hundreds of bombs leaving the

An Apprenticeship to Life

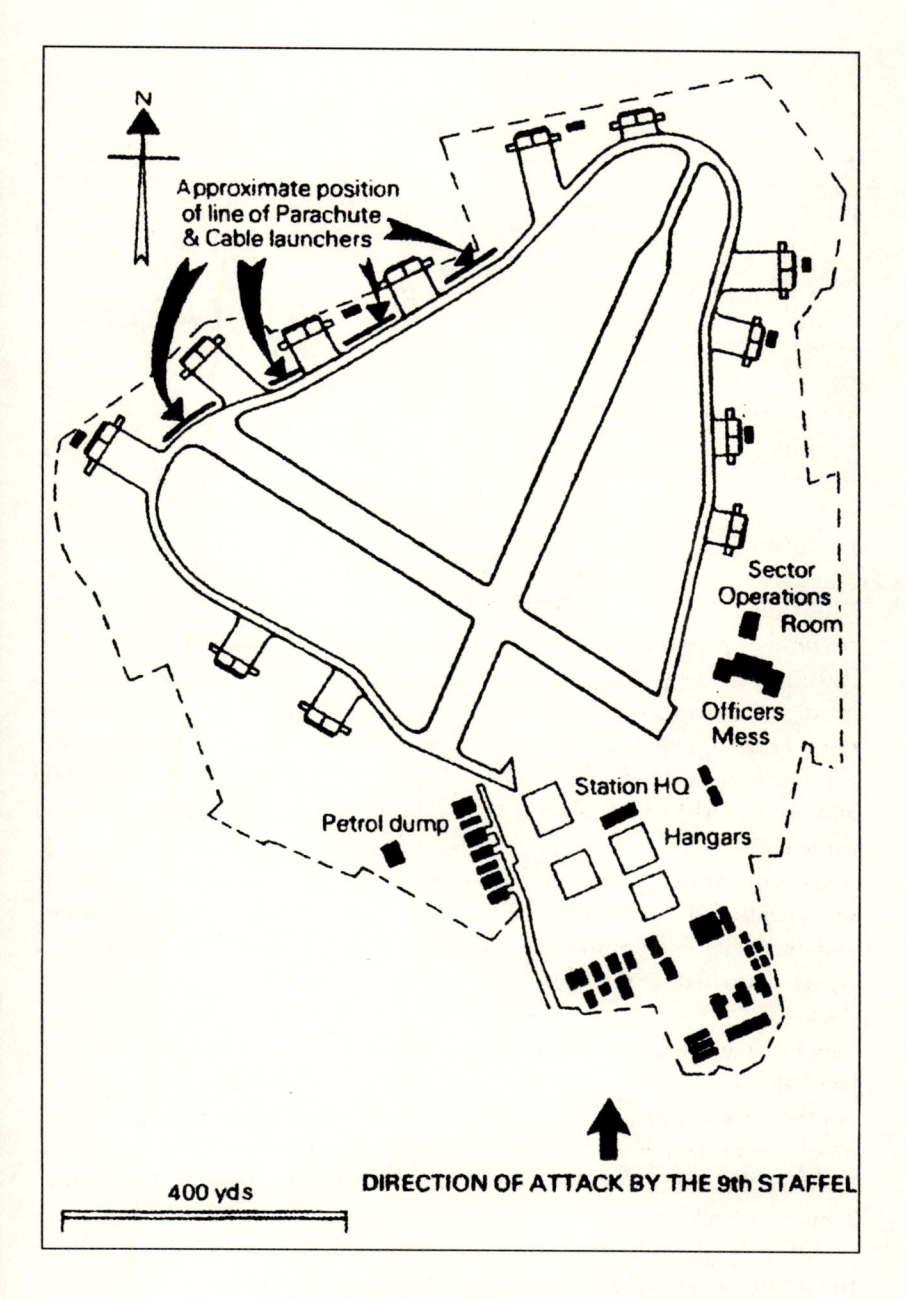

Plan of Kenley airfield circa 1940

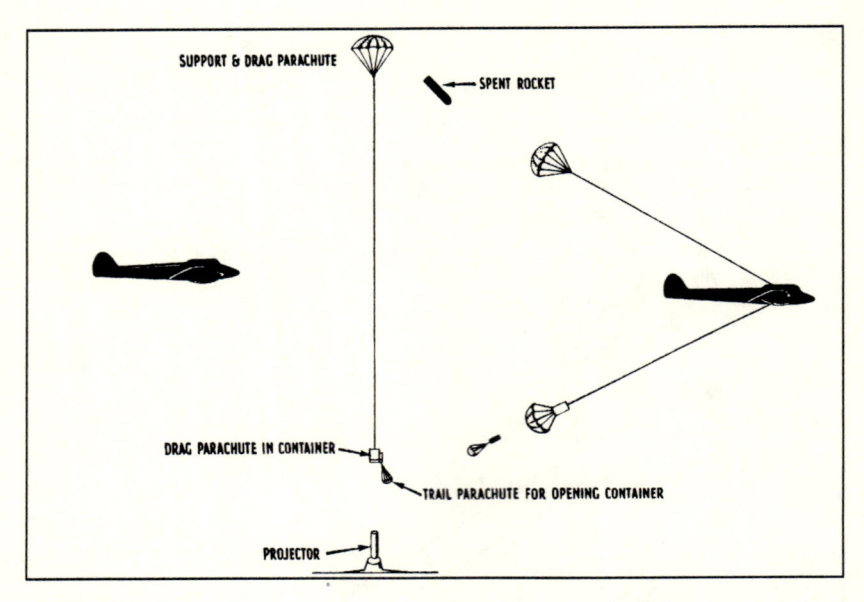

The drag papachute used during the Kenley air raid 18th August 1940

'planes. We watched it all, not wishing to miss anything on this day of days. Little did we know that this was the Luftwaffe's final bid to smash the southern airfields and the R.A.F. On this day the enemy lost 100 aircraft and the R.A.F. lost 136. These losses in one day were never exceeded.

At the time of the raid, there were 12 Spitfires of 64 squadron serviceable, 5 unserviceable. 16 Hurricanes serviceable of 615 squadron, and 6 serviceable. Hurricanes of 111 squadron with 7 unserviceable (Croydon based).

The German force consisted of the 9 Dornier's that carried out the low-level attack plus the sixty that carried out the high level attack. 150 bombs were dropped on Kenley during that day, to us lads it seemed much more. 6 civilians were killed and 21 seriously injured, of the 9 low-level bombers, 4 were destroyed, 5 were damaged and of the 5 only 1 made it back to its base.

Of the high level bombers, 5 were damaged and 5 were destroyed. 12 British fighters were destroyed and 3 damaged. 501 squadron was hit the hardest with 6 fighters lost, 1 pilot was killed and 3 injured . Three of the four hangers were gutted, station H.Q. was wrecked, so were the sick quarters, 9 soldiers and airmen were killed and 10 injured. Aircraft destroyed were 4 Hurricanes, 1 Blenheim on the ground, and 2 Hurricanes and 1 Spitfire were damaged. 4 non-operational aircraft were destroyed and 1 damaged.

Exactly as the people of Brighton stood on Devils Dyke and watched the smoke rise from the burning Crystal Palace only 4 years before, so they stood and watched the smoke rising only 30 miles away from Kenley airfield.

In spite of the 150 bombs, of which 24 were unexploded and the massive damage caused, Kenley was operational within two hours.

As for ourselves we were untouched, our tent was flattened, the slipstream of the crashing Dornier may have caused this and it had a tear in it. Also our Primus stove had a jagged hole in it, this was easily repaired later. We recovered bewildered and scared but highly elated that we had been a part of it all and as near to the action as we ever could have been. What tales we told when we got home.

Getting home was another story, because of the rockets with their parachutes seen high in the sky the police and Home guard were alerted. Soon the area was swarming with forces looking for a rumoured 500 German Paratroops, we had packed our gear and were on our way to Purley to catch the Tram home. Before we left the common we were stopped a couple of times and asked what we were doing on the common.

We never returned to Kenley again knowing that nothing could ever be as exciting as we had seen on that day of 18th August 1940. This had been our baptism of direct attack, we had been closer to the action that afternoon than most people in South London up to that time. It made us not to be afraid of bombs and guns in the years to come and when we joined the forces we were so full of confidence. For one 18 year old, two fifteens and myself at 15½ years, whatever else happened in the future this had been our day.

CHAPTER 9

AIR RAIDS –
THE L.D.V. AND THE HOME GUARD

AIR RAIDS

When the night bombing intensified father was transferred from vehicle washer to full time Firewatcher. Under a new legislation firewatchers were compulsory on business premises at night. Father's colleague George Crouch covered the daytime watch, after the depot closed at 6 p.m. George stayed on until father started at 7 p.m.

On the night of 30th December 1941 I went with father round to the depot about 6.45pm there was a raid in progress, some high explosive bombs had been dropped locally, we did not know where. We arrived at the depot, here I must explain that the depot fronted Acre Lane and was opposite the 'Hope & Anchor' and nearly next door to the 'Duke of Wellington' so it was father's delight. The tea warehouse was at the rear of the three-story building. The lower floor was occupied by a trading company, the first floor was a dancing school, which in spite of war was still open and the top floor was occupied by a shirt making company, with rows of sewing machines with a blacked out roof over the floor. The view from the top parapet was clear across London, the night before was when the City burned around St Paul's. My father, George and I, together with as many pub regulars who could climb the steep stairs watched the fire of London through most of the night. A sight that I will never forget, we could not know of course that the next evening would be our turn.

When we arrived at the depot, George, father and I chatted for a while and just before George was leaving we heard a peculiar plopping sound, at least ten or twelve. George opened the door of the office and just outside there was a burning incendiary bomb. George quickly dumped a sandbag on it, there were seven more burning we took on one each, but four had fallen into tea stacks. Each stack was ten bags wide and twelve bags high and contained 28,800 x ¼ lb. packets. Tea burns with a dense acrid smoke and leaves a very sticky deposit. Father alerted the Fire Brigade who quickly arrived, we were told by them that bombs had already broken the watermain. It was fortunate that the engine had a full tank of water which they used to put out the tea fires. We now turned our thoughts to the fleet of vans at the rear of the depot, there were 21 x 1ton Commer vans, the vans were always loaded the previous evening in order to disperse the stocks of tea. We could not get out of the rear of the depot therefore we had to make our way through the depot once more and go out a side entrance. This led to a long alley way running down to the back. When we got to the rear we found the Kia-ora fruit squash factory burning as well as one of our vans, an incendiary bomb had gone through the roof of the van, through the seat and into the petrol tank which was under the seat, there wasn't much left of the van.

We ran back to the depot and up the side stairs, the dance hall was flooded from the hose and sprinklers, at that stage it was not on fire. The band members and the dancers had fled without even an offer of help; such is the power of self-preservation. The top floor was now burning fiercely, we found that our 2-inch hose had full pressure and away went father and George with the hose. I was standing at the foot of the stairs waiting for the shout 'Turn it on', only to see the coupling disappearing up the stairs. I couldn't make them hear me so I pulled on the coupling only to have them pull it back up. I then pulled the other half of the hose out of its reel to find it was at least a staircase length too short, we often wondered if, had the hose been long enough would we have been able to put the fire out. From the fierceness of the flames, I doubted if we could have stopped the fire spreading.

As it was the fire burnt it self out and didn't spread to the lower floors, probably because the sprinkler system was working well, We never found out why the sprinklers worked and yet the mains was dry. We then went out onto the roof, there was a burning bomb barring the way which father and George dealt with by using the stirrup pump, this was the first time we had used this most prolific of war instruments.

As we stood looking for a way over the roof to reach another small fire two more incendiaries crashed through the depot roof and we knew then we had to get the vans out of the depot. We had to save the fleet of vans, Bill Douglas had told me that the tea could be replaced but the vans were irreplaceable. Father could not drive but George and I could, although I was not old enough to have a licence Bill had taught me to shunt the vehicles around the yard. In fact I could drive better backward than forward, George ran the vans from the yard to the front gate and then I ran them round to the nearest side turning. We rescued all of the vans and the contents of about 12 tons of tea.

We three then stood in Acre Lane, which by then had been closed to traffic and watched the roof burn itself out. The business on the ground floor together with the dance hall and the shirt makers on the top floor never again reopened. Lyons had the depot repaired, it was soon reopened for business and all our jobs were saved.

The whole of the time the building was burning we had an audience from the two pubs, the 'Hope' opposite and the 'Duke' nearly next door. There was no end of help and encouragement from the locals; one even poured his pint of beer onto a burning incendiary lying in the road. It of course exploded, as these bombs were prone to do when doused with water, he remained drunk, even the bang didn't sober him up. Fred Farmer, the publican of the 'Hope' kept us supplied with drinks and sandwiches, and even looked after the firemen. Acre lane was kept closed until the debris had been cleared and the building was checked for safety.

There was a further complication in that someone reported to one of the firemen that in Ashmere Grove, the next turning on the right from the depot something had dropped through the front door of an empty house. All these houses had a front doorstep with a circular metal plate cover that opened into the coal cellar. The step, the door and the righthand brick pillar had been demolished leaving a gaping hole. The fireman went down to the cellar and said there was a complete unexploded incendiary canister buried in a pile of coal. We heard from a bomb disposal expert that it contained 30 x 1 Kilo incendiaries. The barrier across Acre Lane was extended to Ashmere Grove. Had these all ignited in the cellar there would have been a major conflagration. All the bombs were handed out one by one, then the canister was lifted out and the whole was taken to Rainham Marshes and destroyed.

The next few days were spent in cleaning up the depot, all deliveries were suspended and all salesmen and boys with the depot staff were hard at it clearing up. The roof was made safe, a new office and a new workshop with a small staff room had been prefabricated at Lyons Building Dept' at Greenford, and with day and night working it was erected within a week, new bins were made on site, fresh tea supplies were delivered. We were now back in business. Best of all as I had now been permanently for a year with Bill, I now had my own bench to work at, as the new workshop was a little larger than the old one.

The main front of the building was uninhabitable until after the war although the gateway through had to be used for access. I went up to the top floor on many occasions, especially at night to get up on to the roof when air raids were in progress, the views when fires were burning in central London were tremendous. As I passed through the fire wrecked top floor it was an uncanny feeling seeing rows of ruined sewing machines still on the tables. I wondered what became of the girls and women who worked with them. Did they get other jobs, how many survived the war, were any of them in the dancing club on the night of the fire.

Although I had seen many fires and bombing incidents on the rounds with Bob Hare around the docks, little did I think that it would come our way to Brixton. But it did and many times afterwards.

About three months later George, father and I met in the 'Duke' for a quick drink before father took over from George, I was officially too young to be in a 'pub but as long as I wasn't drinking alcohol a blind eye was turned. A warning had sounded at 6.30pm and a couple of 'planes had gone over when suddenly we heard a bomb dropping, we threw ourselves flat on the floor, I had been standing near the flap in the bar top and I slid down between the two ends. The bomb exploded very close, the floor seemed to raise at least 6" and drop back again. Doors were blown in and windows shattered, flying glass cut some people, but no one was badly hurt, certainly all were shaken. I thought, for all my dreams of glory they can stick this for a living.

Father was first up from the floor and he thought of the depot, the three of us left the 'pub crunching over the beautiful Victorian etched windows now lying broken the floor. We passed through the door, and I have a distinctive memory of the air being full of dust, almost as thick as a fog. Father said it reminded him of the German gas on the western front during the First World War, we made our way back to the depot that was only 100 yards away.

As we reached the new gates which had been replaced due to the fire only weeks before, I was behind father and George was standing in the porch of the ground floor shop.

Father put his key into the Wicket gate lock when we heard another bomb falling. Again we threw ourselves flat, there was a deafening bang, there was a terrific blast of wind up the alleyway and then a rush of air the other way, and I felt myself rolling over and over and came to rest at least 20' from the gate, father was propped up against the wall of the alley, he had his eyes shut and was completely still, I feared for him, he opened his eyes and uttered one of his favourite sayings, " cor, bloody blimey, boy that was a one'er" we both stood up and then promptly sat down again with our backs to the wall until we could regain our feet. George came staggering down the alley and said "What are you two doing down here?" father replied "'aving a rest I didn't get much sleep last night". I looked at father and laughed and told him to look at his helmet, the front rim was curled back, he looked at me and said "look at your own", I took it off and there was a great dent in the top. I had a bruise on the top of my head growing nicely so much so that I couldn't put the helmet on until I found half a brick and bashed the dent out. We went back to the Lane and found a lot of the customers from the pub looking for us. One of them said the last he saw of us was when we were in front of the gates. Then he saw the gates hurtle across the road, George said that from the doorway where he crouched he saw the gates fly across the road and drop in front of the 'Hope'. Fred Farmer from the 'Hope' came over with a bottle of Scotch and a couple of glasses and poured some out then gave one to me, I had never tasted whisky before, I swigged it down, it was like another bomb going off, father of course had a second helping. After we had established that we were all present and correct we then went down the alleyway to find that the bomb had landed precisely on top of the temporary office that was built 3 months before, after the fire. The crater was about 15' deep and 25' wide, not a big bomb by the size of the hole. The glass roof had collapsed, roughly half of the alley wall which formed the sidewall of the depot had been demolished, the entire rear of the depot had vanished. If George hadn't left the depot early to meet us in the 'Duke' he would have been in the office when the bomb hit it, and conversely If father and I had met George in the office, all three of us would have died. We stayed on duty until the building security squad came from Cadby Hall.

The next morning we arrived to find the Min' of Food men had arrived and had condemned all tea stocks. As when we had the fire we were allowed to take some tea at our own risk. For some time that evening I did nothing but fill pillow cases with tea, and this time I made sure that no 'Bobby' was going to see me. The same system of repair was adopted as when the depot was burned.

The previous day a 20 ton articulated trailer had arrived from Greenford depot and had been uncoupled to be unloaded, the bomb blast had tipped the trailer up on end, just like a clock tower, the roof was opened up and the tea with difficulty was unloaded. We thought that one day we would see a skilful operation when the trailer was lowered to the ground. Came the day for the recovery, the breakdown truck simply put a chain around the top and pulled, and down it came with a crash. It was cut up on site and taken away as scrap metal.

The depot became operational again but on a much lessened scale, some of the older salesmen like Bob Hare were retired and the depot could no longer retain a mechanic and his trainee (me) therefore Bill was transferred to Normand Ltd at Park Royal. This was Lyons repair factory; I was sent to finish my apprenticeship to Lyons Heavy Goods Vehicle Maintenance at Farm Lane, Fulham. I stayed there until I was called into the Royal Navy in late 1943. I saw Bill from time to time, we both agreed that our moves were beneficial to both of us.

The early 1 Kilo bomb was safe and easy to handle; it had a simple impact fuse and was made of magnesium, which burned, fiercely with a bright bluish white light. I once threw one out of a house by grasping the tail fins even though it was burning. I most certainly had a contempt for these weapons; they were about 2" in diameter and 12" in length. The enemy realised that the bomb was easy to extinguish so it was fitted with a small explosive charge. We soon found that if one smothered it with a sand bag as soon as it ignited there was no harm, but if it ignited and had been burning for a few minutes then it was best left alone until it exploded and was then dealt with.

The magnesium had a peculiar very pronounced smell which lingered long after it was extinguished. Whenever one had burnt out it left a white patch which took a long, long, time to vanish.

Whenever I saw a fin sticking out from a pile of sand I picked it up and put it in the box that I had on the back of my bicycle. Any magnesium that was still attached to the fins I would cut off with a hacksaw, I then cut the rest into small pieces. These were ideal for bringing to life a smouldering fire, a couple of small pieces then the fire would soon be blazing.

Another good use for the bomb was to make cigarette lighters from the metal; I made and used one for many years until I stopped smoking in the early 60's. Although a metal, it could easily be polished to a high degree, my lighter is still around in the house, it must be 61 years old now.

Nasty things happen due to war hysteria, our local greengrocer had a round with his horse and cart, his wife served in the shop which was on the corner of Acre Lane and Strathleven Road next door to where we lived with Uncle Jim before the war. He served the best quality fruit and vegetables; his trade standing was first class. Alas this standing collapsed when war broke out, and all because his name was Tunesi, he was born in Italy. When war was declared he was terribly treated by the local population, especially by a local political party who baited him for some time. He had swastikas painted on his door and some windows were broken. He lost customers but would not close his shop, the awful part of this story was that he had fought with the allies during the first world war and had won an award for gallantry, but this meant nothing when the forces of innuendo got to work. It was reported later in the local press that he had been exonerated from any alien tendencies. It was months before his customers drifted back. He eventually sold his business and retired in the 50's, the shop was still a greengrocers when I last saw it in 1954. The shop was damaged during the war but was always open. He did some small household removals at weekends. There was a strange anomaly in the Vehicle 'C' Licence that allowed a greengrocer to carry coal or do removals, many greengrocers were the first people to change their businesses over to Removal Contractors, during the war it was much more profitable to do so.

THE L.D.V.

It was a chain of circumstances that led me to become a private in the L.D.V. (Local Defence Volunteers); I was about 15 years old and had been working nearly a year. I had made up my mind to buy an air pistol before they were all sold out for the duration of the war or became banned. I duly went to a bicycle shop in Landor Road, Stockwell and

An Apprenticeship to Life

bought a 'Diana' pistol for 7/6d, ironically this was of German manufacture.

Two others of the gang went and bought similar pistols, we set up a range on a bombed site and became fairly good shots. I loaned my pistol to a friend who was trying to persuade his father to buy him one, he returned with the spring broken. I made so much fuss that he promised to replace the pistol, he did. He came round one day and gave me something wrapped in a piece of rag, it felt too heavy to be an air pistol, I unwrapped it and it was a real pistol. We identified it from a library book as a short barrelled 9mm Luger. His father had brought it back from the First World War as a souvenir and had given it to his elder brother who had just been called up. His father had told him to get rid of it because of the war situation. I was naturally the envy of the lads, but as one pointed out 'what was the use of the gun if we had no bullets'. Another said the Germans were still using the same ammunition, we all said that that was a useless piece of information. Another lad said that he could get some bullets as he used to work at the shooting gallery at Brixton and a lot of the bullets were left in the store when it was closed down. He still had a key to the rear door. He turned up one night with a pocket full of .22 short bullets; they were much too small so we were back to the beginning. I had made a dummy cartridge out of a piece of brass rod, I wondered if I could drill and ream a hole through the dummy to fit the .22's, I did and they fitted. That evening we all went up to the bombsite, I loaded the gun, pointed it at a piece of wood and pulled the trigger, and it fired. The bullet went into the wood about ¾", Success, of a kind, we had over 100 rounds and we decided to be the keeper of the gun in turn. All went well for a while until the inevitable happened, one of the lads fired it in the street. Someone local thought the gun was making more noise than a toy gun should and reported it. Our local Bobby investigated it which meant that as he knew us he knocked on our doors in turn. The end result was that we appeared before the Balham Magistrates. The Beak listened to our stories then talked to our parents, he made it sound as though half of the youngsters in the district were running wild with guns in their hands. However the weapon was confiscated and we were directed to report to the L.D.V. Drill Hall in Elm Park Rd where we would get all the instruction we were interested in.

We duly reported to the Platoon H.Q. and filled in a form all stating that we were over 17, and so we became Privates in the Kings Royal Rifle

Corps L.D.V. later to become the1st London Battalion Home Guard. Strangely though, our old Luger was one sidearm more than the platoon had.

The next three months were spent learning foot drill, lectures on weapons and all the excitement that we could want. I was called into the duty office one evening where the platoon officer told myself and two others that we had been checked and that we were found to be under 17 years old and that we would have to leave, A blow indeed. It was suggested that we should apply to the Air Training Corps, we duly did only to be told our educational attainments were insufficient. So we ended up as runners for the A.R.P. at Clapham, just as standbys really just in case the 'phone line between Clapham Common and Clapham South was broken. Those who had cycles were lucky they had no running to do. I had one incident though; I was doing a training run on my bike and had arrived back at the post just off the common. I had propped my bike against the railings of the house alongside the post, the warning had sounded and aircraft were overhead. We heard a bomb drop and explode a bit too near, when we went outside we found my poor bike had suffered a fatal blow, a large chunk of the parapet of the house had fell on the bike and it would never again be fit to ride. To my surprise, a few days later, I reported for duty and the senior warden took me round to the rear of the post and presented me with a bicycle. It was painted bright red with a white serial number on it. It was explained that this was one of a number that had been allocated to the A.R.P., one of which had been sent to Clapham, so it was mine. It was a much more rugged machine than my old one which for later Home guard use was very suitable, more of that later. The rest of my time with the A.R.P. seemed to consist of cycling past the Gun site on the common just as they fired, I put up with the bombing with no problems, but when the guns fired they scared the wits out of me. Oh, the other memory was of the copious amounts of tea I brewed.

As soon as I was 16 I enlisted with the Home Guard (as it was now called). Again I put my age once more as 17 and this time heard no more of it, probably because recruits were sorely needed, I stayed with the HG until I was called up at the end of 1943.

It was soon obvious to the platoon sergeant I had learned foot drill before, this was soon sorted out after a chat and I settled in nicely.

An Apprenticeship to Life

The Guns on Clapham Common that always went off when I cycled past on ARP duties.

Company HQ was at Flodden Barracks in Flodden Road, the Territorial Drill Hall. My Platoon post was at Loughborough Junction Station, Coldharbour Lane, Brixton. From the Lane there was a short passage way to the station. At the end of the passage there was a store belonging to Southern Railways, it was used to store ropes and tarpaulins. There was a large room and a smaller room leading off. The larger room was to be used as a general room, with a small desk and two telephones, one was a general 'phone, the other was direct to Company HQ, there was a mess table and half a dozen chairs. The inner room had three doubles over and under bunk beds. From the railway people we obtained all the paint we needed to paint the place out and turned it into a veritable home from home, to me with my unholy home situation, it was just that.

The weapon I was issued with was a Canadian made 1914 pattern Ross-Remington .300 rifle; an accurate weapon with which I became proficient. This rifle had the loudest bang of any rifle in use at that time. The regular army rifle, the Lee-Enfield Mk2 and the Mk4 were quiet by comparison. This was due to the Ross using black gunpowder and the Lee–Enfields using stick cordite, the smells of the propellants were totally different.

The Home guard gave me the discipline that we all needed, It gave me pride of appearance, and above all it gave confidence in oneself, not that I needed much of that to top me up. It also prepared me for entry into H.M.Forces; it made it easy compared with those who were called up straight from school.

As already mentioned we were N° 1 Platoon 'B' Company, 3rd Battalion Kings Royal Rifle Corps Home Guard. Our Sergeant was an Officer in the First World War, some said he had been a Major. He was good, very efficient, very understanding, he was a man of good stature, his age was unknown although we thought he could have been in his mid 60's. His job in life was as the Foreman of the local dustbin collectors.

Whenever we came off patrol he always had a hot cup of cocoa on the stove and sizzling bacon rashers frying in the pan for a delicious sandwich. Often there would be an egg or a sausage, we never found out where he obtained so much rationed food, although we guessed at a relative who was a farmer whom he visited regularly.

I reported most nights as a stand in for those with families who wanted a night off. I usually reported in around 8 p.m. Our patrols were in the railway area, up and down the marshalling lines. I was not fond of these patrols, they were too open and at night the lines shone like a beacon. The only way to stop them shining was not to use them and let them rust.

We carried out a patrol of two hours on and four hours off. This was carried out from 6pm to 6am; seven nights a week, because of a permanent understrength two of us were on duty nearly every night.

The was a diversion now and again, when a raid was in progress we were recalled from the patrol because of the danger of wagons loaded with ammunition, there was one track spur that was isolated from the others, we were always suspicious of any wagons that were parked there. During the raids we often got call outs to help in the locality. One such incident was when a land mine exploded over Barrington Road one night. We were asked to help to retrieve an elderly man from his shattered house we duly trotted to the site and there he was still in bed on the first floor, but the front wall of the house had disappeared! The floor was at an angle of 30° and the only thing holding the bed to the floor was the fact that the back legs of the bed had passed through the floor. We could see that the two flights of stairs were intact but the landing in between was just a gaping hole. The two rescue men were loathe to go up the stairs, they were built like bullocks, it was thought that the weight of the two would be more than the stairs would stand, so myself and another of the HG were asked to go up, which we did. We dragged two planks up and bridged the hole, then up the next flight. The door was jammed, we called for a crow bar which we pulled up with a rope, the door was ripped off easily, then we could see the old chap, he had slid down the bed and was huddled at the foot against the bed rails. I made my way across the floor which was actually springing up and down, I was able to reach down and get the rope under his arms and made my way back to the stairs where I felt much more safer. The rope was passed down the stairs to strong arms and we began to pull.

The old man began to holler like blazes, he was refusing to let go until someone found his potty that was under his bed. Like hell we thought 'all together boys, PULL, and they did, he came off the bed, onto the sloping floor and up to the door. We grabbed him and laid him on a stretcher which we had pulled up, he was strapped in and lowered down, not once did he appear grateful. He went away in an ambulance swearing at the top of his voice about his pot. His daughter thanked us all; we said she was welcome to him. We didn't realise we had a audience of neighbours until we heard clapping a cheering as the old man came out of the door. Neighbours told us that he was a nice kindly man, Hmm.

We patrolled in pairs; there was always two out and four in. Our sergeant came around at times just the make sure that we were doing our job. During the winter it could be very cold tramping the railway lines, there was the occasional sound of rats scampering across the lines and disturbing the ballast between the sleepers. Then on a cold night there was a cracking sound of the rails contracting as it became colder, the few passing trains made a terrific noise but on raidless nights it became very, very quiet. On one such night we heard a tapping sound, very similar to a Morse code machine being operated. We alerted the post and they came out to us, our sergeant split us into groups and we advanced up each side of the line of wagons that the sound seemed to be coming from. We had been alerted that during the day before a Heinkle, bomber had been shot down. Three of the crew had been captured and one was still missing after bailing out over South London. Now we were creeping along the line and we heard the tapping coming from a wagon only two ahead. We rushed and flung the doors open, nothing, but the tapping was still going on, it was coming from a brake block quietly chattering on a wheel, the line sloped at this point, whoever was suppose to put the brake on didn't do their job properly. We thought that if we hadn't caught the airman, we might have caught a looter. At that time looting was prevalent from the railway.

I liked the moonless nights when in a clear sky we could see a myriad of stars, our sergeant was also knowledgeable in the study of the heavens and often gave us impromptu lessons of the various star formations. I was amazing what one could learn in the Home Guard. If the Germans had captured us I am sure that they would not have had the knowledge of the stars that the 'B Coy' boys had. It was during such a session that I realised how valuable a pair of binoculars were and what a large amount of light they pulled in at night.

Most of us had bicycles to move around on, the rifle was a cumbersome thing to have slung on ones back when cycling, my firm was making half track vehicles for the army, which had rifle clips fixed behind the two front seats. It occurred to me that these clips would be ideal fitted to a bicycle. On my next visit to the Park Royal factory for stores items, I managed to 'Borrow' a dozen clips. Having become a proficient welder and metal worker it was easy to fabricate brackets to mount the clips to a bicycle crossbar. Shortly afterwards our small unit carried our weapons clipped to the bikes between our legs. The word passed down the line and soon the Company Lieutenant saw them and mentioned them to Battalion HQ. Whereupon our bikes were inspected, because the clips were painted khaki it was obvious that they were Government Issue, and we expected to be reprimanded, but as our sergeant said, "They can't sack us". He was right as usual, shortly afterwards clips were offered to all Home Guard units, large sighs of relief.

This had been a period of immense effort, after the depot was bombed the garage had been closed and I had been transferred to Walham Green (now Fulham Broadway.). Because of the uncertainty of public transport each morning after a night of bombing, I decided to travel to work by bicycle, about five miles each way. Because of the pressure of Home Guard duties I was seldom out of uniform, many times I didn't go home for days. It was work to home Guard and Home guard to work. Sleep was the greatest enemy. At lunch times, those who were in the Home Guard or the A.R.P. could be found in groups dozing. Yet, on the rare night that I was off duty, I helped out the fire watching at Acre Lane depot with my father. I was not yet 17 years old with a wealth of war experience behind me, and still 1½ years to go before I would be called up to do my 'bit' for King and country.

CHAPTER 10

OUR POLITICS – MOTORCYCLES – CALL UP

OUR POLITICS

As youngsters in the intermediate pre-war years we were not interested in politics in a formal sense, Labour, Conservatives and other parties and their doctrines were just so much mumbo jumbo to us.

The party however that gave us much excitement was Oswald Mosley and his 'Blackshirts', in the years 1936 and 1937, Mosley and his British Union of Fascists were on the ascendancy and were holding meetings through the country. Their local meeting place was in Venn Street, Clapham, near The 'Plough' clock tower. The meetings were publicised by posters stuck on walls and windows. The local Communists and members of the National Unemployed Workers Movement (N.U.W.M.), which were communist dominated usually held their meetings in the same or near by streets. There was much barracking between the two factions and often fighting broke out. Sometimes the fighting was organised.

We lads attended the meetings and watched from a discreet distance just waiting for trouble to break out, and for the police to move in. We loved to see the mounted police in action. Of course our parents forbade us to be there but we made excuses and were just nearby.

Some meetings were held in Lambeth baths, one of Mosley's senior men often spoke there, he was William Joyce. Joyce had a distinctive scar on his face; it reached from his mouth to his right ear. This was caused by a razor slash at a Lambeth meeting in the early 20's, I only saw him once, and I would never forget his face. Mosley put up Joyce for the L.C.C. elections in March 1937 in the Shoreditch Division. He gained 2,564 votes compared with the successful candidates 11,098. Mosley later used falling finances as an excuse to be rid of Joyce. At the outbreak of war, Joyce fled to Germany and joined the Nazis; where he became famous for his broadcasts in English, with "Germany calling", "Germany calling". He was captured in 1945, was found guilty of treason and hung. He was only 40 when he died. However, back to the meetings. Venn Street gatherings usually started with a march up Clapham high Street. The Black Shirts were always immaculately turned out and well disciplined, they had a sprinkling of thugs who were the bullyboys for defence.

There was always barracking from the crowd, invariably planted communists, speakers stood on a rostrum and always had things thrown at them. At one meeting on a Saturday afternoon the argument developed into a pitched battle, after the mounted police moved in the fight carried on down the High Street and on to Clapham Common and then around the Old Town. Often we did not know what fight to watch first. I distinctly remember seeing police, Blackshirts and 'Commies' struggling in the new children's paddling pool near the Old Town. How bewildered we were as well as excited, could grown ups really behave like this? Are these the people who aspire to run the country? Yet our parents were so placid and did not really want to know the truth behind the scuffles and riots that went on less than 1 mile away.

In one way the coming war was a blessing in disguise; this seems a terrible thing to say when one considers the millions who died. But, and a very big but, if war had not come along this nation could well have been governed by the Fascists or perhaps the Communists, and could have been subjugated forever.

During the battle all sorts of weapons were used, clubs, sticks, knuckle-dusters and the favourite, a milk bottle with a piece of thick string tied around the top. The milk bottles of those days had a wide top with a thick lip and were twice as thick as the bottle of today. They could inflict a nasty injury and could be dropped without any evidence of ownership.

The worse fight was in Cable Street on the 4th of October 1936. Forever called 'The Battle of Cable Street'. The communists, to prevent the Blackshirts from holding a meeting erected street barricades. Fighting was prolonged and vicious, in all 83 were arrested and of these 83 all were anti-fascists, it would appear that Mosleys supporters were well behaved or clever, in fact on of the leaders of the battle against Mosley was one of the most violent Communists in London. In this fight 70 people were injured.

I recall father talking to his friends, they were very worried that the fighting would turn into Civil war, this was the talk for many days afterwards.

Cable Street seemed to have been the climax of the bid for power by both the Communists and the Fascists and it was nearing the outbreak of war. Mosley and his union were in decline, after the war broke out he was interned in the Isle of Man, together with his wife. There was a fear of the role he would play should there ever be an invasion.

After the war Mosley was released, he reformed his party under a new name the 'Union Party', this never succeeded and he passed into obscurity, he emerged now and again with a public outburst which usually had good logic in its content.

We followed Mosleys career in South London just for the excitement of it, we knew not of what he stood for, nor did we care, and now after all the past years I think many of his supporters had the same attitude as we had.

The Communists of course existed throughout the war and have caused problems since. I also think it is safe to assume that the British people are not of extreme political motivation, nevertheless, we had fun and excitement, but all in all we thought they were just a bunch of loonies.

MOTORCYCLES

Bill Douglas taught me to drive when I was 16½, we would drive out to St Paul's Cray and Sidcup via Crystal Palace, and there I would have practise drives along lanes free of traffic. Long before I was 17 I could drive competently J. Lyons & Co Ltd's Austin 12 van. Those weeks of learning to drive were happy weeks indeed. There were no tests during the war, all tests were suspended and only provisional licences were issued, so as soon as I was 17 I obtained my licence.

When I moved to Farm Lane depot after Brixton Garage was closed I worked with an excellent mechanic, Fred by name. Fred was motorbike mad; he had a 500cc Norton 'Cammy' International in immaculate condition. After being there for a month or two I heard of a motorbike for sale in Farm Lane, Fred and I went to see it, it was in a deplorable state and was in an old shed at the side of the house. As soon as Fred saw it I could sense that he was dead keen that we had it, we pulled it outside and saw that it was a Rudge Ulster 500cc. From the fact that it had neither kickstart lever on it, nor a decompression lever it was obvious it had been used in its day for competitions. We haggled on the price and I bought it for £1.10s. I had a bargain. We pushed it down to the depot and put it in the bay where we kept our bikes and bits. Over the next few months it was stripped down and overhauled. The original tank was Rudge red, which we were able to match and the frame was stove enamelled black, it looked good. Many parts were re-chromed and we even had the chain case cover repolished.

Came the day to start it. The accepted way was to pull it back in gear until it was on compression, hold the clutch lever in run and push the machine, jump into the saddle and as your weight comes down let go of the clutch lever. It should have fired and it didn't. When I was 17 I was very slim and weighed only 8 stone, and this was just not heavy enough to push start a bike like the Rudge. Fred started and ran the bike; it certainly sounded a dream. I needed a kick start and a decompressure lever and the bits for it. The bike stayed at farm lane for some time except for the few times when Fred ran it around the block. I arrived at work one day and there on my bench was a Rudge cylinder head and a gearbox, dirty but complete. No one knew any thing about it, it had just appeared, and of course we set to and cleaned and fitted the parts. Now I could use it, and well use I did, I had great joy for a few months. The tax for the bike was £1.6.3d a year and the insurance was £1.10.0d a year. My glorious days with the Rudge were all too brief when soon afterwards came my call up. A few weeks afterwards I met an old friend who worked at Claude Rye in Fulham Road. After chatting he said "Did you find the Rudge bits I left for you", I was so surprised that it was he who had left the parts, he said that there was no one in the workshop, so he just left on a bench, It just happened to be my one. Apparently he was clearing out a bombed motorcycle dealer that belonged to Claude Rye and he removed the pieces from a smashed Rudge. He wouldn't even let me pay him for his kindness.

When I joined the Navy I simply left the Rudge in the car store at Farm Lane where Lyons laid up vehicles for the duration of the war. I had a few spots of leave and went on each occasion to check my bike and found it OK until I was posted abroad. A year later when I came home and visited my old work place, I found the Rudge missing, it was never found.

I had many happy times with motorcycles after the war years before I turned to the comforts of a car but all this is outside these formative years and its story.

CALL UP

On the 3rd of May 1943, I received a letter from His Majesty's Government inviting me to the Enlistment Board. I had to attend at the Territorial Drill Hall at Tulse Hill, South West London. I reported on the due date and had a medical examination and was graded A1. I was asked for a preference for which force I wished to join, I asked to join the R.E.M.E. (Royal Electrical and Mechanical Engineers) as I was serving an apprenticeship in Heavy goods vehicle Engineering. I was told I would serve in the R.E.M.E., and in due course I would receive my enlistment papers. In about two weeks I received a letter stating that I had been deferred for 6 months because of my apprenticeship, I was asked for a second choice and gave The Royal Marines as a Landing Craft Mechanic. A few months later I received my calling up papers and after another medical examination, still A1; I was told I would be entering The Royal Naval Air Service as an Air Mechanic. So, there we are, First the REME, then the Marines and finally into the senior Service, where I was to fulfil all my dreams of travel which I have described in earlier chapters.

I had served my Apprenticeship and had qualified to enter the world of responsibility toward my country my family and my fellow men.

I reported for duty at H.M.S.Gosling at Warrington, Cheshire, on the 3rd of November 1943. Now perhaps I could get on with doing something to help end this war.

THE EPILOGUE

When I finished my training I was given 7 days leave. Not wishing to spend a week with my inebriated parents or an undecided fiancé, I thought why not go some where else and enjoy myself. for some reason I thought of Filey, on the Yorkshire coast with its lovely beach, it came to mind because of the LNER poster with the invitation 'Come to sunny Filey'. I duly queued for my travel warrant; I was asked where to, Filey I replied. I was given a railway warrant to Filey and return to

Cannock. I was taken to Cannock station in a camp truck along with about 20 others. I changed trains at Sheffield and arrived at Filey with a couple of quid and some loose change in my pocket, I had all my needs in my small navy attache case, the case was a standard issue, my kitbag and hammock were left in the hut at Hednesford.

At Filey I enquired at the police station for the address of the local YMCA, this I was told was within walking distance. On signing in I was grateful to find that all was free, a bed each night and all meals. Over the next few days I really enjoyed my own company, and not that I wanted to scrounge a drink, I found that there was always someone saying " Have this on me Jack". Yes, I still have good memories of Filey.

Then came the day to return to Hednesford, and using my warrant I arrived back in good time, I reported in and gave my number and name. The RPO looked at me and said, "What are you doing here"? I said "Well I went on leave from here and I am reporting back", I was told that a telegram and a travel pass had been sent to me to return to Bedhampton Camp and why wasn't I there? I asked where was the telegram sent to, to your home address was the reply, But I haven't been home said I, and I explained that I had not been asked for a leave address. I could imagine that this could turn nasty with me ending up on a charge or something or other, He looked up the warrant book and found my issue and on the copy was just a line across the page. "Right" he said, "You had better get yourself to Bedhampton" he was writing as he was talking " Here is another warrant, the truck will take you to Cannock Station". I thanked him and said that I would collect my kit and hammock from the hut, he told me that everyone's kit had been sent already.

Now, Hednesford is in Staffordshire, and Bedhampton is near Portsmouth in Hampshire, normally a train journey of 6 hours, but taking into account any air raids it could be longer I believe it was near Doncaster that we stopped in a tunnel and moved on as dawn broke. After changing trains in London I arrived at Bedhampton Halt station in late afternoon the next day, there was a line of transport waiting, I climbed into the first one and was taken to the camp, where I duly reported to the RPO's office. I gave my rank number and name, The PO looked up and said "What are you doing here, there is a search going on for you", I thought Gawd, here we go again. He disappeared into an inner office and returned with a young Sub/Lt, "Ah, Bannister " he said, "What are you doing here", I felt like giving him a two finger salute, doing a smart about turn and marching out. On reflection I thought this might aggravate the man so I should humour him, so all bright and breezy I related the whole story, then I realised it was getting longer and longer. "Well " he said" your lot left here yesterday with your leading ranks and you are supposed to be at Gosling 3"

Now, N° 3 Camp, H.M.S. Gosling is near Lowton St Marys, Warrington, in Cheshire and it is where I did my basic training when I was called up. I was told to doss down for the night and was also confined to camp for the night, I think they were afraid they may lose me again. I was given a chitty for a supper and breakfast the next morning; I asked for an advance of pay and was given £2.10s.

The next morning I asked about my kit. I was told it was on its way to Gosling. I was give a ride to the station in the usual truck and had a two-hour wait for the next train to London. I arrived in London in the middle of the afternoon during an air raid. I took the underground to Euston station; the next train to Warrington was just before 7am the next morning. I now had two choices, One. Go home for a few hours, or two. Find the good old YMCA, while having a 'cuppa' at the station I thought it would not be a good thing to spend an evening with that dreadful family of mine, there was bound to be a row over something silly, so the YMCA it was to be. I had a good meal, the dormitory house was nearby, and I had a wallow in a nice hot bath and was awoken in time for breakfast. After which I walked to the station, and this time I did manage to find a seat on the train, the entire bill for the YMCA was 1/9d!

After a horrendous journey of 13 hours that went right along the Welsh coast we arrived at Warrington, there had been no sustenance, no heating and as many standing as there were sitting. The usual trucks were waiting; one of which took me to the camp. So, once more I reported to the RPO, I waited for it, and I surely got the question "What are you doing here" it was dawning on me that I wasn't wanted, and if they kept this up it would shorten my war service. I replied "Can you please tell me where I am supposed to be", "Why do you ask" was the reply, I once more repeated the whole sorry story "You are absolutely right "said he "You are supposed to be at Potter Heigham". I thought Christ where's that, I was told it was on the Norfolk Broads. I went again through a familiar pattern, Get a meal, find a bunk, no it's not here, your kit has been sent on, go and get another warrant and off on another train.

An Apprenticeship to Life

I arrived at a small country station where every siding line was full of box wagons; these were being loaded with equipment for MONABS, Ah, that is the subject of my first book. Once more a truck took me to an ex-RAF airfield near the small village of Ludham, I was driven round the perimeter track to a site. As I entered the site office I saw my C/O Lt Topping," Ah Bannister" he said "Where have you been", I very nearly put myself on a charge, I said to myself have a bit of decorum Harry, and decorum won the day. Oh yes, I did find my gear.

THE END